I0407932

*PRESERVATION IN AMERICAN
TOWNS AND CITIES*

To Virginia and Zachary

PRESERVATION IN AMERICAN TOWNS AND CITIES

Nathan Weinberg

Westview Press / Boulder, Colorado

All rights reserved. No part of this publication may be reproduced or transmitted in any form or by any means, electronic or mechanical, including photocopy, recording, or any information storage and retrieval system, without permission in writing from the publisher.

Copyright © 1979 by Westview Press, Inc.

Published in 1979 in the United States of America by
  Westview Press, Inc.
  5500 Central Avenue
  Boulder, Colorado 80301
  Frederick A. Praeger, Publisher

Library of Congress Cataloging in Publication Data
Weinberg, Nathan.
    Preservation in American Towns and Cities.
    1. Historic buildings—United States—Conservation and restoration. 2. City planning—United States.
    I. Title
    E159.W4   069'.53'0973   79-83
    ISBN 0-89158-488-9

Printed and bound in the United States of America

CONTENTS

FIGURES

FOREWORD

"Diversity" is the word to describe the preservation movement today. After the decades of saving presidents' birthplaces and war heroes' headquarters, the preservation movement has leap-frogged into alliances with environmentalists, developers, and merchandisers. Following an era during which preservation was equated with patriotism, the movement today is fused into governmental goals for energy conservation, urban social improvement, and jobs.

Historic preservation in America has arrived.

Bankers are teaming up with historians to find money for neighborhood revitalization. Developers are hiring restoration architects to turn musty old buildings into profitable businesses. Investors and tax accountants are seeking out technical consultants to insure both architectural integrity and maximum economic benefits from their investments in preservation. Lawyers, lobbyists, and lawmakers have joined the museum curators, historical society members, and "don't-tear-it-down" protesters to save and reuse America's built environment.

The sophisticated preservation techniques pioneered in Charleston, S.C., New Orleans, and Santa Fe are being adopted by uncounted thousands of neighborhood groups and nearly six-hundred landmark and historic-district commissions throughout the country. The pursuit of excellence exhibited in the restoration and reconstruction of Colonial Williamsburg is being studied and, with new purpose, being drawn on for "Main Street" revitalization programs in hundreds of cities and towns. Our landmarks—both the extraordinary and the everyday ones—are being recycled as living, contributing buildings and places that enrich our lives.

Ten years ago it would have taken a long search through cadres of urban demolition experts to find the one or two officials at the U.S. Department of Housing and Urban Development who knew or cared about historic preservation. Now not only is there an emerging preservation consciousness among HUD officials at the national and regional levels, but preservation has an equal footing with other environmental and social issues as a consideration in all HUD-financed projects. Other government agencies, too, have developed preservation policies, plans, and departments.

Elected officials are realizing the popularity of the preservation theme. If preservation has not yet been accepted as a basic planning tool by every mayor, city council member, and county commissioner, it seems no longer a matter of "if" but of "when." Annual meetings of the National League of Cities now include a preservation seminar. Smart politicians at all levels of government have picked up preservation almost as fast as they picked up property tax reform.

The parade, however, still lacks recognition as a national priority. The new level of activity is remarkable but tax laws, codes, and pressures for growth keep us short of a "Preservation Ethic." That is our challenge.

It does bear noting that the argumentativeness of the movement is diminishing in the face of this public acceptance. Preservationists who had grown accustomed to their own raised voices and table thumping are now less shrill. They have begun to research and evaluate their own accomplishments and to express concerns for quality in their projects and their organizations. A new confidence is bringing changes. Preservationists who plaintively used to deliver press releases to news rooms now find themselves being interviewed by business and real estate writers, and have learned to shift from aesthetic appeals to bottom-line shrewdness.

Two aspects bear noting: There are large numbers of young people coming into the preservation field and they bring not just the traditional credentials in art and architecture, but degrees in law, social science, planning, landscape, and business. And their eyes tend to cast new values on art deco theaters, early gas stations, twentieth century boats, diners, and drive-in hamburger stands from more recent years.

Further, the young make us realize that the field has become increasingly professionalized. There are jobs in preservation. The volunteer has not disappeared. Quite the contrary. Now, even larger numbers of volunteers are joining professionally staffed preservation organizations.

An understanding of what has happened in the preservation movement in 130 years—from the spacious lawns of Mount Vernon to the row houses of Mount Auburn in Cincinnati—is important. As this book shows, not all the problems have been solved nor all the fights won, but the momentum is magnificent. The biggest problem now is to be democratic in a field that was once dogmatic and to practice common sense in an area that was once largely academic. But the momentum—still growing—is our golden opportunity: It is sufficient to give us time to study our own progress and to continue refining our standards, identifying our weaknesses, and extolling excellence in the new marketplace of preservation.

Robertson E. Collins
Vice Chairman, National Trust
for Historic Preservation

PREFACE

Historic preservation refers to the activities of those who attempt to save architecturally significant buildings from destruction. They are moved to this effort by the hope of perpetuating a tangible record of the civic past. Preservation serves economically to recycle old structures, socially to revitalize communities, and symbolically to link the culture of the present to that of the past through the juxtaposition of their architectures.

We have only recently begun to glimpse the potential of urban preservation. For many years we thought of historic preservation as an activity of the social elite. In part this is true, but today's preservationist seeks a broader role for preservation. Reflecting on the urban clearance programs of the last decades, the public monies wasted on destruction of a spirited and sturdy past and construction of a uniform and shoddy present, on cheap and socially disastrous low-income housing projects, one cannot but suppose that preservation and restoration may be better ways to treat the urban fabric.

In city after city preservation has made headway, and the public is often enthusiastic with the outcome. Municipal leaders are gradually accepting preservation as a criterion for city policy; to a certain extent the state and federal bureaucracies have done so as well. However, governmental support of preservation as an urban policy has been limited because of the frequent displacement of low-income residents from restored areas, and because of the increased demands for municipal services from such areas.

To a preservationist, public and private assistance should be provided to low-income neighborhoods to aid the residents in upgrading their houses, and municipal services to the neighborhood should be on a par with those in other parts of the town or city. Residents of deteriorated neighborhoods have argued that they would be better able to reverse deterioration if public services were provided equally to all neighborhoods. At times, they have also argued that architectural preservation and restoration are not a necessary part of renovating their neighborhoods. Since the middle and upper classes do place a value on preserved historic architecture, the poor may feel that preservation would displace them from their neighborhood. However, displacement or gentrification occurs because restoration is usually found only in a few desirable neighborhoods. If preservation were a policy for the city as a whole, then displacement would occur less often.

As the preservation movement has expanded in recent years, a variety of new problems have appeared. Any reader of *Preservation News,* the newspaper of the National Trust for Historic Preservation, is aware that increasing attention is being paid to matters of real estate development and speculation, displacement, transportation, planning, and innovative programs—matters at one time tangential to preservation and restoration. In this study the various cases illustrate these problems in order to relate preservation to social and economic conditions in different locales. No attempt is made to exhaust the examples or deal with all aspects of preservation. For instance, Beacon Hill is discussed as an example of neighborhood preservation; it could also have been discussed as an historic district, but other cases were more informative. Furthermore, aspects of preservation activity that are well understood are not dwelt upon; there are already many excellent discussions on how to do an architectural survey or on the technical details of restoring a building. Instead, by examining the materials both historically and in terms of specific issues, I attempt to put preservation in perspective as a social activity. By knowing what is possible and what has been achieved in various preservation contexts, we can be more judicious in our choice of goals and more successful in reaching them.

ACKNOWLEDGMENTS

I am indebted to the many preservationists, planners, architectural historians, public officials, and private citizens across the country who shared their time and knowledge with me. I remember and appreciate their courtesy and encouragement.

I should like to thank Virginia Alexander for research assistance and for editing the manuscript, and Dr. Arthur Lane for additional editorial advice. Part of the research for this book was supported by a grant from the Mabelle McLeod Lewis Memorial Fund.

1. AN INTRODUCTION
TO HISTORIC PRESERVATION

It has not been unusual in our culture for some old buildings in a state of disrepair or ruin to be set aside and restored as historical monuments. The appreciation and study of monuments and ruins are not peculiar to our time, but an active preservation movement is of recent origin. Perhaps no one has presented the sentiments of this new movement so eloquently as William Morris before the Society for the Protection of Ancient Buildings in 1884:

> Surely we of this Society have often had to confess that if the destruction or brutification of an ancient monument of art and history was "a matter of money," it was hopeless striving against it. Do not let us be so feeble and cowardly as to refuse to face this fact, for, for us also, although our function in forming the future of society may be a humble one, there is no compromise. Let us admit that we are living in the time of barbarism betwixt two periods of order, the order of the past and the order of the future, and then, though there may be some of us who think (as I do) that the end of that barbarism is drawing near, and others that it is far distant, yet we can both of us, I the hopeful and you the unhopeful, work together to preserve what relics of the old order are yet left us for the instruction, the pleasure, the hope of the new.[1]

For Morris, the purpose of historic preservation was the protection of ancient monuments of art and history from the barbarism of the present moment.

The word *monument* has an elaborate meaning; the *Encyclopaedia Britannica*, eleventh edition 1910-1911, defines it as:

literally that which serves to keep alive the memory of a person, an event, or a period. The word is thus applied to a column, statue, or building erected for that particular purpose, as "The Monument" (i.e., of the Great Fire) in London; to all the various memorials which man throughout the ages has raised over the buried dead, the barrows and cairns of prehistoric times, the representation of the living figures of the dead, brasses, busts, &c., or the varying forms, allegorical or otherwise, taken by the tombstones of the modern cemetery. In a wider sense "monument" is used of all survivals of a past age, in which sense it may include all the vestiges of prehistoric man, dolmens, menhirs, remains of lake dwellings, stone-circles, and the like, buildings large and small, cities, castles, palaces, and examples of domestic architecture, which have any interest, historic or artistic as well as movable artistic or archeological treasures, which exist in private or public collections, or which are discovered by excavation, &c.[2]

G. Baldwin Brown, in *Care of Ancient Monuments* (1905), suggests the change in meaning that preservationists brought to the term *monument:*

> We must of course dissociate the word from its common use as applied to public memorials of departed worthies, such as the Nelson Monument in Trafalgar Square, or the Scott Monument in Edinburgh. The care of such monuments is invested in officials responsible for public order . . . whereas the offences against ancient monuments which people of good taste and piety are always trying to prevent, are perpetrated by people on their own property, and without any criminal intent that the ordinary law can recognize. When we speak of "monuments" and the "care of monuments" in the sense in which the words are used in these pages, a far more extensive collection of objects is in contemplation than the public monuments noticed in the guide books. Roughly speaking all old structures, and all the objects we preserve in museums, are included for the present purpose under the term.[3]

He continues:

> The monument is something that gives us pause, that bids us reflect, and is a reminder of past or absent things. In this sense the extended use of the word is as justifiable as the narrower. The Wellington Monument in St. Paul's brings before us the thought of "the man who

fought a hundred fights" and who sleeps below in the vaults, but equally does the Roman milestone or the Gothic cathedral make us think of the men who marked their irresistable march by the former, or breathed their religion into stone in the other's majestic pile. These relics of old time are monuments because they recall, not this or that named and famous personage or group, but the whole life with all its associations of some period or place of which the interest is in the past.[4]

Because of its older connotations, the term *monument* has never been fully satisfactory to preservationists, and therefore they have used many other terms: *historic buildings, historic landmarks, cultural heritage, cultural property,* and *historical and artistic sites.*

In general, monuments fall into two categories: those that are intentional and those that become monuments after the fact. The former are the triumphal arch, the mausoleum, the obelisk, the pyramid, the megalithic monument, the sepulchral brass, the burial mound, the tomb, etc. Many of these were originally forms of propaganda. They reflect the earlier connotation of monument and the historic period in which the ability to make a large architectural statement indicated power. Furthermore, while conquerors have burned cities and slaughtered their inhabitants, their fear of dead spirits frequently saved tomb monuments from destruction (if there was a treasure in the tomb then it was another matter).

Monuments after the fact, which reflect the extended meaning preservationists have given the term, are historical, artistic, or natural and are chosen according to criteria that have gradually been developed as the movement has changed. In establishing these criteria, preservationists have considered several questions: What is historically significant, what is artistically significant, how old does it have to be, has it been moved or reconstructed, and is it feasible to preserve it? (For a modern set of criteria see Appendix F.) Modern criteria leave considerable room for interpretation; and although they indicate the kinds of structures it is desirable to preserve, they do not indicate the procedure by which a particular house is chosen for preservation while others are neglected. Consider, for example, a recent preservation: "Schoolchildren file into the Frederick Douglass home, 'Cedar Hill,' in Washington, D.C. It was dedicated as a national shrine and opened to the public

February 14. The papers of the influential black abolitionist (1817-95) recently were placed in the Library of Congress."[5] Reference to the criteria alone will not explain either the sudden national recognition of the Douglass home, or its tardiness.

Monuments, as evidence of history, require both academic and popular interpretations. Thus preservation shares in the common assumptions of modern academic history, archeology, and art history; and yet also shares in the workings of earlier forms of oral history, myth, legend, chronicles, and genealogies, which have persisted in the popular world. Children are acquainted with family genealogy and family history at the dinner table, legendary and mythical events are recounted during the religious holidays, the chronicle of the nation is related in the grammar school, and the sites of historic events can be visited during vacation. Scientific history disenchants the world for those who have learned its viewpoint, but popular understanding has not absorbed the scientific perspective consistently though it is often fascinated by it. An art historian once recounted the story of his childhood visits to the church of Hagia Sophia in Istanbul. Although the church had become a museum, for his father it remained a sacred building surrounded with legends. The boy learned these legends and came to see the church in that light; only many years later after a formal education was he able as an art historian to see the building stripped of its legends, replete with the facts of its construction and style.

For the modern historian, the scientific account is no doubt preferable to the mistaken chronicle, even though other modes of historical explanation must also be considered as they bear upon historic preservation. Scientific history finds its origin in the philological method:

> Such a method consists of verifying the source of evidence and decomposing it: that is to say, before accepting evidence, one tries to determine upon what it is founded, and then decomposes this source into its original separate sources. This external process of criticism of sources accomplished, one passes to the internal process: that is to say, one seeks to determine if and to what extent the author of the evidence has reason to tell the truth or to modify or falsify it.[6]

Though modified, embellished, and at times challenged, this method has remained a model for historical scholarship; however, the formal and technical conventions of this method have in practice limited its appeal to a small learned audience. Popular history, on the other hand, although it sometimes uses the methods of academic history, has not excluded elements of legend and myth in its presentation of past events to the public.

In most cases historic preservation makes use of a combination of scientific and popular approaches. In a well-done project the restoration of a building or site frequently relies upon an examination of the available sources following the prescribed academic method. Descriptive accounts, paintings, drawings, photographs, and building records are examined. The building techniques of the period are studied, and the site is excavated to find the original foundations. Paint is scraped from extant walls to find the original color, and old furnishings are located or replaced with replicas made from studies of period furniture. The entire apparatus of the historian, architect, and archeologist can be brought to bear to produce an accurate restoration.

However, much of this scientific effort is not often explained to the visiting public; instead the forms and techniques of popular history mediate between the historic site and the public. Displays are set up to present a general interpretation of the historic events that took place, and tableaux are used to suggest the appearance of the site during different activities. Guides recount the dates and circumstances of foundings, battles, and destructions; and tales and stories relating frequently mundane occurrences help bring the history home. Patriotic legends surrounding national figures, wars, civil wars, treasons, and treacheries are represented, while in most cases crime, corruption, and other evidences of social deprivation are excluded from the harmonious picture. Finally celebrations, processions, dances, or meetings may be reenacted in their original costume and setting. At Williamsburg, one may hear the heroic words of Patrick Henry spoken again in the hall of House of Burgesses: "If this be treason, make the most of it." For popular history, at its best, everything is as it was, and "you are there."

Naturally preservationists also seek historical precedents for their activity. Jacob Morrison, writing on preservation law, notes that Gibbon offers some evidence of preservation efforts during the rule of the Roman Emperor Majorian (453 A.D.):

The monuments of consular or Imperial greatness were no longer revered as the immortal glory of the capital: They were only esteemed as an inexhaustible mine of materials, cheaper and more convenient, than the distant quarry. . . . Majorian, who had often sighed over the desolation of the City, applied a severe remedy to the growing evil. He reserved to the senate the sole cognizance of the extreme cases which might justify the destruction of an ancient edifice; imposed a fine of fifty pounds of gold on every magistrate who should presume to grant such illegal and scandalous license; and threatened to chastise the criminal obedience of their subordinate officers by a severe whipping and the amputation of both their hands. In the last instance the legislator might seem to forget the proportion of guilt and punishment, but his zeal arose from a generous principle, and Majorian was anxious to protect the monuments of those ages in which he would have desired and deserved to live.[7]

Morrison also mentions efforts by Theodoric, who was "appalled at the pace of destruction." Another writer on preservation, Stephen Jacobs, devotes the first chapter of an extensive work on American preservation and its antecedents in Europe to preservation "from Hammurabi to the French Revolution." However, most of his discussion concerns the city planning efforts and monumental building compositions in this long period. A notable occurrence of preservation activity during the Renaissance is included in this survey:

The Scholarly Pius II was the first Pope to publish a Bull intended to protect the old public buildings of Rome and its environs, relics which he had personally investigated. Published in 1462, it provided for the fining of individuals caught damaging antique remains. In the first quarter of the sixteenth century, before the sack of Rome, we find great interest in preservation at the Papal court. Thus, in 1515, Raphael was able to persuade the first Medici Pope, Leo X, to issue an order forbidding the destruction of antique marbles with inscriptions. However, only a few years later (1518-19) he was forced to report that those who were appointed to preserve the ancient remains were often the principal despoilers of them. He might well have pointed to Pius II, who ignored his own Bull, taking from both the Colosseum and the Capitol for his new constructions. Under such conditions, attempts to protect ancient remains must have been of more theoretical than practical value.[8]

The sentiment for preservation during the Renaissance, the rediscovery of Vitruvius's treatise on architecture and the study of the ancient orders by architects, the sketching of ruined buildings and the drawing of conjectural reconstructions all display an admirable appreciation for the past; but they do not constitute a preservation movement.

Many of the ancient buildings that have come down to us partially intact survived not through any intentional antiquarianism, but through their conversion into churches. The Roman Pantheon "was transformed into a Christian church in the VII century . . . saved from destruction and spoliation. Several popes ordered restorations, but its original lines were left unaltered. Unfortunately Pope Urban VII used some bronze decorations from the ceiling, the portico and the tympanum for the canopy in St. Peter's and the guns in Castel S. Angelo."[9] The Great Mosque of Cordova was preserved through the now notorious act of building a cathedral in its middle, and it is a favorite pastime of tourists and art historians to search out a view that excludes the Christian elements. Given the field of vision of the human eye this is practically impossible, but photographers with a variety of lenses have been more successful, making it possible for tourist shops to offer the purist a book on either the mosque or the church. Both the churches of Saint Bernard and Saint Mary of the Angels in Rome were built with portions of the Baths of Diocletian; however, Christian remodeling of the interiors predominates. Other baths in the city and the market of Hadrian remain because of their durable concrete construction though their marble facings are missing. In all likelihood, the preservation in these cases was fortuitous, the outcome of maintenance through use, or endurance despite neglect.

There are other antecedents of the preservation movement that are perhaps more closely related to it than those usually discussed. The first is the keeping of relics. These sacred objects were carefully preserved in special cases, handled only by professionals though they might be touched by pilgrims; sometimes entire chapels were devoted to them. The Sainte Chapelle in Paris was built to hold the crown of thorns, and a chapel was built in the Topkapu palace in Istanbul to hold Islamic relics taken from Cairo when it fell to the Ottoman Turks. In the latter case, the shift of the relics legitimated a shift in the center of religious authority in the Islamic world from

Cairo to Istanbul. A description of the kinds of relics found in one chapel, the Church of the Blessed Virgin in the Great Palace of Constantinople, was written by a participant in the Crusaders' conquest and sack of the city (1204):

> This chapel was so rich and so noble that no one could ever tell you its great beauty and nobility. Within this chapel were found many rich relics. One found there two pieces of the True Cross as large as the leg of a man and as long as half a *toise,* and one found there also the iron of the lance with which Our Lord had His side pierced and two of the nails which were driven through His hands and feet, and one found there in a crystal phial quite a little of His blood, and one found there the tunic which He wore and which was taken from Him when they led Him to the Mount of Calvary, and one found there the blessed crown with which He was crowned, which was made of reeds with thorns as sharp as the points of daggers. And one found there a part of the robe of Our Lady and the head of my lord St. John the Baptist and so many other rich relics that I could not recount them to you or tell you all the truth.[10]

After the sack of the city, these and other holy relics were dispersed to the churches of the West where they can still be found. It is in the special treatment given to relics and in the ways of distinguishing pieces of the true cross from ordinary wood that modern preservation and museum techniques are anticipated. In preservation sacred objects of religious nature have been displaced, in large measure, by revered objects of an historic and secular nature.

Relics were not, of course, the only objects collected before the rise of the public museums and of historic preservation in the nineteenth century. In an attempt to classify the forerunners of the modern museum according to their social function, Alma Wittlin has suggested the following categories: (1) economic hoard collections, (2) social prestige collections, (3) magic collections, (4) collections as an expression of group loyalty, (5) collections stimulating curiosity and inquiry, and (6) collections of art stimulating emotional experience.[11]

Wittlin presents examples of each type of collection, which for the most part fulfilled more than one function. The collections of the Greek temples included votive figures of an expensive and prestigious nature, national memorabilia of reputed Homeric origin, and curiosities from distant lands possessed of magical properties. The extensive collections of European monarchs usually served for any social function necessary, though the emphasis of the collection shifted with the taste of the period and the character of the king and his ministers. While Philip II of Spain gathered an immense collection of relics, Louis XIV and Colbert invested in paintings, and Emperor Rudolph II in Prague sought to transmute baser metals into gold in his cabinet of globes, tools, games, and curiosities. Each had as well rooms of treasure, magical medicinal stones, ancestral portraits, Roman coins, bronzes, tapestries, etc. The diversity of social functions served by such collections is only indirectly determined by the objects themselves: it also depends on the use or display of the collection in recognized settings and on the social position of the collector. The emulation of the great collectors by great numbers of people of limited resources in the last century and a half has made possible the collection of almost anything that has grown scarce. However, it has not entailed a corresponding diffusion of social function beyond the influence exerted on the narrow circles of family, neighborhood, and acquaintance.

The presentation of specimens in the great collections was made in several different ways. When not on display in a decorative ensemble, in a learnedly or geometrically arranged gallery, or as the framework or background of a performance, the specimens were frequently kept together in an eclectically arranged storeroom. In scientific collections curators attempted to classify the specimens according to raw material, the method of Pliny's *Natural History;* not until the nineteenth century did the classificatory principles with which we are familiar become common. Only on special occasions were elements of these premodern collections displayed to the public; with the exception of temple and church displays, the collections were for the rich.

In analyzing the evolution of historic preservation, commentators often discuss three nineteenth-century European cases that offer a comparison with American experience; these are the French, English, and Scandinavian variants. French preservation naturally begins with the French Revolution. In the republican and anticlerical fervor of the times, churches were stripped of their interiors and some were pulled down, émigré property was seized, and the possessions of the king were nationalized. The painting gallery in the

Louvre was reconstituted as a national museum, and a Commission of Monuments was established by the National Convention to oversee the art works acquired from the church property nationalized in 1789. The art works were stored at the former convent of the Petits-Augustins while the commission sorted through them choosing items for the Louvre. Alexander Lenoir, who was in charge of the depot,

> used his office as guardian to lay claim to the paintings, sculpture, tombs, and ecclesiastical furnishings that the Commune of Paris was stripping from the churches. By his energy and zeal, Lenoir saved much from vandalism, from the lime-pits, and from the state's foundry—he camouflaged the bronze statues with plaster.
>
> The Commission of Monuments asserted its claim to the paintings and these went to the Louvre, but Lenoir kept the sculpture, church furnishings, and stained glass. He then systematically arranged the objects and fragments chronologically and installed in separate rooms what he had classified according to periods and designated by style "Merovingian," "Carolingian," etc. By the nature of these installations, he contributed to the notion of the evolution of art.[12]

Lenoir has kindly left an account of the inspiration for his novel arrangement:

> At the opening of the Royal Vaults in the Abbey of St. Denis, I had an opportunity of making many interesting observations. Several of the great personages, who in the early centuries had been interred in stone sarcophagi, were found with their clothes perfect, and with various other articles which had been used by them whilst living. These objects of antiquity, important in establishing the chronology of costume, were unfortunately broken to pieces and conveyed to the Mint.
>
> Such a considerable Collection of Monuments of every age struck me with the idea of forming a regular, historical, and chronological Museum, where a succession of French sculpture should be found in separate apartments giving to each Salon the character and exact fashion of the age it was intended to represent; and of removing into other establishments the Paintings and Statues, which had no immediate connection with either the French history or that of the arts in France.[13]

In October 1795, after the Committee of Public Instruction had approved Lenoir's plan, the depot at the Petits-Augustins was designated the Musée des Monuments Français, and remained so until 1816 when the restored monarchy ordered the dissolution of the museum and the return of the collections to the church. Nevertheless, the influence of the museum continued through the circulation of engravings Lenoir had made of the various rooms.

An attempt was made by the revolutionary government to promote the inventory and listing of monuments through the work of local agents, but this was not successful. In the Napoleonic period, after the concordat with the pope, the church regained many of its buildings and undertook their maintenance. In 1810, Count Montalivet, minister of the interior, ordered the departmental prefects to list chateaux and abbeys and to report on other monuments and works of art. Between 1810 and 1818 the ministry received 100 replies, and between 1818 and 1830 another 485.[14] Nevertheless, the listing of monuments did not become fully effective until after 1830.

Two other innovations appeared during the revolutionary and empire periods. The first was the museum of Madame Tussaud, perhaps the originator of historic simulation, whose work has remained popular and has stimulated competitors to attempt comparable feats in other media. The response of the public to historic simulation, which is treated as entertainment and distraction (such as the Disney parks, Busch's Old Country, and Knott's Berry Farm), provides a social counterpoint to the seriousness with which historic preservation is approached. The second innovation came at the end of the empire when "the sense of history of the era led to the preservation of an interior for public display because of its associations (one of the first instances of this procedure). For many years the bedroom in the Palace of Fontainebleau from which the Emperor departed for Elba was kept just as he had left it."[15] Preserving, or restoring, an interior associated with a famous person or act in an historic house museum has been frequently adopted by preservationists who feel, in the words of Walter J. Hickel, former secretary of the interior, that "written history, for all its abundant values, cannot instill the feeling that comes from being on the scene itself—standing in the room where a great event transpired and walking in the pathways of pioneers."[16] Obviously an accurately furnished room will help the public to even greater empathy with the past.

Following the revolution of 1830, the government made its

concern with monuments formal by establishing the post of inspector general of historic monuments within the Ministry of the Interior. This renewed concern for monuments reflected a change in French taste in the 1820s, associated with the development of Catholic conservatism by Chateaubriand, Bonald, Maistre, and Lamartine, and of Romanticism by Hugo, Nodier, Delacroix, and others leading to a reevaluation of Gothic buildings: "In the 1820's, accompanying the great renascence of historical studies, there was heard an increasing outcry against the neglect of the country's architectural heritage, in which Hugo and Montalembert denounced vandalism with particular vehemence, while Baron Taylor and Charles Nodier began publicizing the forgotten artistic riches of the provinces in a celebrated series of travel-books."[17] Others who took part in this effort were Alexandre de Laborde, Arcisse de Caumont, founder of the Society of Antiquaries in Normandy, and Guizot, the historian-minister who created the post of inspector general for his friend Ludovic Vitet.

Vitet was inspector general for four years and devoted himself to establishing his small department in the ministry bureaucracy, to the listing of monuments, and to some preservation. In 1834 he left the post to go to another ministry and was succeeded by Prosper Mérimée, who was to hold the post for nineteen years. Mérimée, usually remembered for other achievements, faced difficulties in fostering preservation; to begin with there was a lack of architects with the appropriate training:

> Most of them were completely ignorant of medieval art, and the initial restorations were disastrous. At Saint Ives de Braisne the architect demolished four sections of the nave, the transept that closed western side, and all the sculptures of the facade; at Sainte Croix de Bordeaux and at Lorris the weakened pillars were robed in a thick coating of masonry that hid the defects without curing them; at Saint Remy the architect solved the push of stone vaults by replacing them with wood.[18]

Then there were the untutored actions of local officials who tore down old monuments that were in the way of new developments, or of local clerics who renovated their churches by replacing medieval fixtures with modern neoclassical pieces or by whitewashing murals—practices that had gone out of fashion in Paris. And finally there were squabbles within the government bureaucracy over funds and concerning which department should have jurisdiction over which ancient monuments. Mérimée dealt actively with each of these problems. In addition, he took yearly regional tours to list and describe neglected monuments and to talk with local officials and his assistants. Through Mérimée's efforts government funds for historic buildings increased almost tenfold, and over 4,000 buildings were classified as historic monuments.[19]

The theoretical issues that arose around the subject of building restoration in Mérimée's time have remained central issues for discussion and practice in the preservation movement to the present. Inspector General Jacques Dupont in a recent essay on Viollet-le-Duc, Mérimée's chief architect, has presented what is perhaps the primary issue:

> Monuments, as a rule, have been repaired and enlarged throughout the ages, a fact that creates considerable embarrassment when the original parts and the modified sections need to be restored. Should we neglect the latter and re-establish the original unity of style, or must we restore the whole and maintain the later modifications? The decision in each case depends upon particular circumstances. But in general the decision must take into account respect for the original style, archeological knowledge, and the quality of the addition.[20]

During his career Mérimée approved limited restoration, but not the reestablishment of any original unity that might have disappeared or never been completed:

> When there is some certainty about what remains there is not the least objection to repairing it, or even rebuilding it, but when it comes to supposing, to adding, to recreating, in my opinion one is not only wasting one's time but also running the risk of making serious mistakes and causing others to make them as well. Note that as a science archaeology is still in its infancy. . . . At the present moment I believe it unwise to try to reconstitute something which has totally disappeared.[21]

And yet Viollet-le-Duc, who enjoyed Mérimée's patronage, diverged from this position, particularly in his later restorations to such an extent that at the end of the nineteenth century his work was identified with the "vandalism of finishing."

Viollet-le-Duc achieved early fame for his restoration of the Basilica of Vezelay in 1840, a task that other architects had refused to attempt because the building was likely to collapse. His success led him not only to undertake other restorations, but also to elaborate a system for historical restoration and for architecture that ran to more than eighteen volumes. In this effort his understanding of the techniques of medieval building surpassed that of his fellow architects, and his conception of medieval design in which decoration and structure are unified in an "ensemble" came to influence his restorations. Consequently he and his students began to modify and finish monuments, adding spires, sculptures, suppressing classical decoration and inventing pseudo-Gothic furnishings in a "mania for the unity of style" that was later to be condemned; nevertheless, recent criticism of his work has been tempered by the realization that many of the buildings might have fared worse at the hands of men less sympathetic to medieval architecture. After the death of Viollet-le-Duc and partly in reaction to his methods, a new doctrine came to dominate preservation work: "A monument to be a testimony to the past must stay as the past has bequeathed it. To pretend to restore it to its original state is dangerous and deceitful; we must preserve buildings as they are, respecting the contribution of successive generations."[22] To examine the emergence of the new doctrine we must turn to the English case.

The first formulation of the "antiscrape" philosophy, as it was to be called in England, came from John Ruskin in his early work *The Seven Lamps of Architecture* in 1848. Of restoration he wrote in the "Lamp of Memory,"

> Neither by the public, nor by those who have the care of public monuments, is the true meaning of the word *restoration* understood. It means the most total destruction which a building can suffer: a destruction out of which no remnants can be gathered; a destruction accompanied with false description of the thing destroyed. Do not let us deceive ourselves in this important matter; it is *impossible,* as impossible as to raise the dead, to restore anything that has ever been great or beautiful in architecture. That which I have above insisted upon as the life of the whole, that spirit which is given only by the hand and eye of the workman, never can be recalled.

And in the place of restoration he suggested:

> The principle of modern times . . . is to neglect buildings first, and restore them afterwards. Take proper care of your monuments, and you will not need to restore them. A few sheets of lead put in time upon the roof, a few dead leaves and sticks swept in time out of a watercourse, will save roof and walls from ruin. Watch an old building with an anxious care; guard it as best you may, and at *any* cost from every influence of dilapidation. Count its stones as you would the jewels of a crown; set watches about it as if at the gates of a besieged city; bind it together with iron where it loosens; stay it with timber where it declines; do not care about the unsightliness of the aid; better a crutch than a lost limb; and do this tenderly, and reverently, and continually, and many a generation will still be born and pass away beneath its shadow. Its evil day must come at last; but let it come declaredly and openly, and let no dishonoring and false substitute deprive it of the funeral offices of memory.[23]

It was to be twenty-eight years before a preservation society espousing these principles was founded, although the *Seven Lamps* was extremely influential among the Gothic Revivalists who read other sections of the work, and Ruskin was seen by the public as a champion and leader of the revival movement.

In England, and the argument could be made for France as well, historic preservation and restoration emerged in the context of the Gothic Revival. The origins of the revival stretch back into the eighteenth century to Walpole's Strawberry Hill and to Fonthill Abbey, to the picturesque Gothic garden pavilions suitable for terminating a view, to the sham ruins and ruin sentiment taken from the paintings of Salvator Rosa and Claude Lorrain, and to the antiquarian interest in a style that in England at least had never quite died out. As long as the picturesque attitude prevailed in the interest in Gothic, improvements made to the rediscovered Gothic buildings after their long neglect were not burdened with the question of authenticity:

> These restorations were called improvements, and arose from the fact that the eighteenth century's conception of Gothic did not always agree with the evidence of actual examples. It was felt that a certain amount of fretwork, a certain number of pinnacles, were essential to

true Gothic style; and where these were deficient they were added.
Plain surfaces, like those of the old Oxford colleges, were enriched
with shrines and canopied niches, and pinnacles were added to the
towers of Bath Abbey. In the wealthier and more enlightened dioceses
restoration had begun in the 1780's.[24]

After 1800, with the publication of pamphlets, magazines, and books
featuring detailed engravings of Gothic buildings and tracery, the
archeological attitude displaced the picturesque and authenticity was
favored over sham. However, this did not prevent many parish clergy
from decrying the improvements of their predecessors and
undertaking their own "restorations."

The use of Gothic in the building of churches after 1820 added a
moral dimension to the revival that had not been previously present.
This quality was heightened after Pugin published his *Contrasts* (1836)
in which the sordidness and misery of increasingly industrial England
is graphically placed beside the wholesomeness of Gothic England.
The identification of Gothic with a moral dimension continued to
grow with the formation of the Cambridge Camden Society (1839),
whose members "had arrived at Gothic architecture by reversing
Pugin's position. He had said: to revive Gothic architecture you
must also revive old forms of worship. They said: to revive old forms
of worship you must revive Gothic architecture. His impulse had
been primarily architectural, their's was primarily religious; and
since religion is a wider and more exciting topic than architecture,
their theories of Gothic became more influential than his."[25] The
Camdenians not only preferred Gothic, they especially preferred the
decorated mode, which, because it dominated the central period in
the development of Gothic, they felt to be the zenith of the style and
therefore most in harmony with their religious goals. This preference
influenced the Camdenians' views on their second purpose—
restoration:

> There are two ways, said the Camden Society, of restoring a church
> built at different periods: either restore each of the various
> alterations and additions in its own style, or restore the whole church
> to the best and purest style of which traces remain. Of these
> alternatives the Society unhesitatingly recommended the second.
> Now there were few restorable churches in which some fragment of
> "decorated" could not be found. Perhaps there was a porch or a

chancel, perhaps only a window, and forthwith the whole church was transformed to suit it. But sometimes the architect was faced with a church built too late to include any detail of decoration. Should he restore "perpendicular"? Surely not. Surely his manliest course was to pull down the whole church and rebuild it in a real and natural style.[26]

The excesses of this kind of restoration went largely unopposed from the 1840s until William Morris founded the Society for the Protection of Ancient Buildings (SPAB) in 1877.

Incorporating the antiscrape philosophy of Ruskin, the SPAB was successful in changing the techniques of preservation from restoration to conservation. In founding the society, Morris had intended to protect only medieval buildings from restoration, but when Carlyle was invited to join he stipulated that this protection be extended to the Wren churches that were then endangered with demolition. Although Morris cared little for the architecture of the seventeenth century, he could not oppose its protection without endangering his own position; and in this way the purposes of the society were extended to include the prevention of demolitions as well as restorations and to recognize other styles with Gothic.[27]

The work of the SPAB has been augmented by the formation of several offshoot groups, notably the National Trust (1895), the Georgian Group (1937), and the Victorian Society (1958). At present the National Trust is the largest private landowner in England holding a quarter of a million acres of scenic land. The organization of the National Trust's "Country House Scheme" provides for "the owner and his descendants to remain in residence and yet avoid heavy taxation, provided they are able to supply an endowment sufficient to maintain the place and are willing to have it open to the public at specified times."[28] The tax shelter afforded by this arrangement makes upper-class participation in the National Trust well motivated.

Following the lead of the private organizations, the English government has protected Celtic and Roman remains and has incorporated provisions for historic preservation in its Town and Country Planning Acts. Before the close of the nineteenth century most European countries passed some form of legislation to protect their monuments.[29] In France the work of inspectors general was formalized in the Historic Monuments Act of 1887, and in England government activity was acknowledged in the Ancient Monuments

Protection Acts of 1882, 1900, and 1913. In the most recent period, following the Second World War, historic preservation in Europe has become enmeshed with the city planning techniques of historic districts and restrictive zoning; and the aesthetic and historic consequences of changes made in the cityscape or countryside are now incorporated as routine considerations in the decision process of the planners. Furthermore a new body of technical literature about preservation has been generated by UNESCO agencies concerning the conservation of "cultural property" as it is now called.[30] With the exception of war-damaged buildings (a large exception considering the widespread destruction of the last war in Europe), the established approach of modern preservationists is summarized in the "oft-mentioned rule of thumb": "Better to preserve than to repair, better to repair than to restore, better to restore than to reconstruct."[31] In this regard, the professionalized and institutionalized preservationists of today, though benefiting from technical advances, remain within the context of their nineteenth-century predecessors.

A third example of historic preservation occurred in Scandinavia and differed from the previous two cases in its origin and its method. Faced with the decline of Scandinavian craft industries in the late nineteenth century, museum director Arthur Hazelius hoped to stimulate their revival through the creation of an outdoor museum of old buildings where the practice of folk crafts could be displayed. At the Nordiska Museet in Stockholm in the 1880s and later at Skansen, Hazelius developed a series of techniques for the preservation and display of folk culture that have influenced both museums and historic preservation. At the Museet he introduced tableaux in an "obviously theatrical technique where rustic figures in peasant costumes merged into the scenes depicted and where the decorations and furnishings of the rooms were of the same provenance as the costumes. Sometimes these tableaux were actually modelled directly upon realistic paintings by contemporary Swedish artists."[32] At Skansen, the world's first outdoor museum opened in 1891; old wooden buildings from throughout Sweden were assembled and carefully rebuilt in a village grouping so as to suggest an actual village. Although in Hazelius's time peasant settlements were thought to represent the spirit of Swedish tradition, he collected from other social strata as well. Today, most of the more significant types of houses and building techniques in Sweden are represented at Skansen. Besides the peasant farms there is also a manorhouse. Other aspects of the community are represented by a church, market stalls, inns, etc. Nor are these layouts limited to rural settings; impressions of the towns and cities are also presented. From Stockholm and other towns there are a number of typical buildings arranged in the form of a town district with streets and hills. Here besides the usual dwellinghouses there are a number of workshops such as a printing-office, a book-binder's, a goldsmith's workshop, a bakery, a tannery, a shoemaker's workshop, a pottery and a glass-blower's workshop. A number of these crafts including the ancient art of spinning are at intervals demonstrated by skilled craftsmen in these authentic milieux.[33]

The reconstruction of an entire village suggested a holistic conception of preservation that has been followed at Williamsburg and in the establishment of historic districts in many cities.

A final innovation of the Scandinavians was the opening of their museums to the general public:

During the first half of the nineteenth century the keeper of what later became the Danish National Museum sometimes personally explained the contents of the collections to chance visitors, children, and adults who came in straight from the street—this at a period when, at the British Museum, for instance, it was sometimes only after the greatest difficulty that permission was received to be allowed in, and then only after a thorough investigation of credentials.[34]

At Skansen, interpretive programs were developed and guides trained to aid the visitor in orienting to and understanding the buildings and exhibits, and this practice has become a standard, though not always appreciated, feature of museums and historic areas. In preserving the past for future generations, most preservationists did not realize that the future generations might not be interested, might not be able to understand, or might reject the past. The Scandinavians recognized the problem and created the interpretive programs as a solution. However, the problem has remained, if it has not intensified, suggesting that there may be more involved in its resolution than interpretation.

In nineteenth-century Europe there were many centuries-old

buildings that could serve as historic buildings; however, when similar sentiments arose in the United States there were few buildings of great antiquity or significance to preserve. Until the last quarter of the nineteenth century Americans did the best they could with early New England houses, Southern plantations, revolutionary battlefields and headquarters, Indian relics, mastodon bones, and the mounds in Ohio.

The first instance of preservation in the United States occurred in 1816 when the city of Philadelphia bought Independence Hall from the state of Pennsylvania. The state no longer needed the building and before selling the land for building lots offered it to the city. The purchase by the city was motivated by the "strong and impressive recollections" associated with the Old State House, as phrased three years earlier in a "Memorial" that Philadelphia citizens had addressed to the legislature when it first thought of selling the building and land. Unfortunately, before the hall was in the care of the city, two wings were torn down to make way for fireproof buildings (1812-1813), and the woodwork was stripped from the room where the Declaration of Independence had been signed (1816). The city provided a new coat of paint in 1824 when Lafayette visited, a new steeple in 1828, and new woodwork for the Assembly room in 1831 (the Haviland restoration). For a time Charles Wilson Peale's Museum of Natural History, which included portraits of the presidents and the skeletons of a mastodon and an Indian elephant, resided in the hall; however this collection was displaced as the hall became a shrine in favor of the Liberty Bell, a statue of Washington, and other objects of antiquarian and patriotic interest.

The preservation of Independence Hall was not followed by any other efforts until the 1840s and 1850s. An attempt was made in 1847 to save the Old Indian House in Deerfield, the house having at one time withstood an Indian attack, but it was demolished; whereas the Hasbrouck House, one of Washington's headquarters, was saved when New York State purchased it. The legislature's report on the purchase expressed the patriotic sentiments associated with the house:

If our love of country is excited when we read the biography of our revolutionary events, how much more will the flame of patriotism burn in our bosoms when we tread the ground where was shed the blood of our fathers, or when we move among the scenes where were conceived and consummated their noble achievements. No traveler who touches upon the shores of Orange county will hesitate to make a pilgrimage to this beautiful spot, associated as it is with so many delightful reminiscences in our early history, and if he have an American heart in his bosom, he will feel himself a better man; his patriotism will kindle with deeper emotion; his aspirations of his country's good will ascend from a more devout mind for having visited the "Headquarters of Washington."[35]

An effort to save the Hancock House in Boston, which was offered to both state and municipal governments between 1859 and 1863, met with failure. Charles Hosmer, historian of the preservation movement in the United States, suggests that this failure made New Englanders distrustful of preservation carried out through the legislative process, whereas the opposite pattern became established in the Middle Atlantic states where legislative action was effective.

The first nationwide preservation effort was organized by Ann Pamela Cunningham to save Mount Vernon. Cunningham, after a famous letter directed to the "Ladies of the South" and the failure of other attempts, founded the Mount Vernon Ladies' Association, chartered by the state of Virginia to raise money to buy the Washington home from John Washington in order to save and maintain it for the nation. In 1859, six years after the letter appeal, the association succeeded in purchasing the house; the methods employed established another pattern for preservation:

The leader of the movement . . . had been a believer in publicity, for it should be remembered that she valued newsmen as allies in her work. In addition, the grand tour of Edward Everett had served to bring the Mount Vernon Association to the attention of thousands of Americans of all ages. Last, but by no means least, the Ladies' Association was not just a group of thirty vice-regents who assembled once a year to hear the orders of the regent; it also included hundreds of lady managers and their assistants. Combine these elements with the unquestioned national veneration for Washington, and one may foresee that the Mount Vernon movement would influence preservationism for years to come. This must have been what happened, for from the ranks of the younger lady managers of the Mount Vernon Ladies' Association were to come the leaders or parents of the leaders of the great wave of patriotic associations in the 1890's.[36]

The Mount Vernon effort influenced work done at Valley Forge and at Andrew Jackson's home, the Hermitage; inspired Mary Longyear, who saved three houses associated with the life of Mary Baker Eddy; and stimulated numerous other groups to save houses that were "second only to Mount Vernon."

Following the Civil War and the centennial celebrations of 1876, the historic preservation movement was well under way. In the last decades of the century the need for the patriotic education of the masses of new immigrants was uppermost in the minds of the Colonial Dames, the Daughters of the American Revolution, and other patriotic groups: "A nation cannot fail of nobility that reveres high ideals, and holds them up for the admiration and emulation of its children. In preserving such landmarks as this (Mount Vernon), in cherishing the associations that belong to them, and in holding them up for reverence of the rising generation, our Societies will find their highest and most compensating work."[37] Aside from patriotic motivations, there were other reasons, especially in New England, for preservation. For example, the Rumford house was saved by the Rumford Historical Association (1877) to preserve the birthplace of the scientist Count Rumford; the Reuben Brown House was saved by the Concord Antiquarian Society in 1877 to house the Cummings Davis collection of Americana; the Hancock-Clark House was saved to hold the collections of the Lexington Historical Society (1876-1877); the Whipple House was saved by the Ipswich Historical Society (1898) for its antiquity and architectural features; the Thomas B. Aldrich House was saved by the Thomas B. Aldrich memorial group as a literary memorial (1907); the Fairbanks House was preserved by the Fairbanks Family in America to save the family homestead (1901-1904); and similarly the Alden and Howland houses were preserved by their respective family associations. As a result of local interest in preservation, the movement was more extensive and successful in New England than in other sections of the country.

While preservation proceeded at the state and local levels, the federal government remained inactive toward buildings until after 1900. During the Civil War the Lee mansion at Arlington was seized by the government, and following the Lincoln assassination the Ford Theater was also seized; however, the Arlington mansion was not restored until 1929, and the Ford Theater waited until the 1960s for a complete restoration. In the 1890s the government established a series of battlefield parks as memorials to the Civil War; but its most creative action was the protection of areas of great natural beauty. As early as 1864 the government gave the Yosemite valley and the Mariposa redwood grove to the state of California to be preserved; and the first national park was established at Yellowstone in 1872. This innovative protection of natural areas established a precedent for other countries.

In this century the emphasis in preservation has shifted somewhat from a historical and patriotic to a cultural and architectural viewpoint. Architects have contributed to restoration work, and the American Institute of Architects (AIA) has preserved the Octagon House in Washington as its national headquarters. Museums have shown an interest in preserving the interiors of demolished houses for use in period rooms although this approach has occasionally brought them into conflict with preservationists who would rather see the entire building saved. The full possibilities of preservation and restoration approached in a holistic cultural, historical, and natural framework have become apparent in the work done at Williamsburg after 1927:

> The miracle of restoration made possible by Mr. Rockefeller and his family, at a cost of $79,000,000 over 41 years, is only now coming to full fruition. Protected by a verdant green belt, the 130 acre historic area today includes 85 restored buildings of colonial date and 49 major buildings, plus many smaller ones, that have been reconstructed. A craft program that began with a handful of small shops in 1939 now represents 30 crafts.[38]

Because most preservation organizations have small resources, Williamsburg remains a unique example of what is possible; it has nevertheless had an important influence on the establishment of historic districts and has demonstrated the attractiveness of revitalized historic structures to tourists. Without the realization of the economic value of the past, such projects of preservation-through-use as the Cannery and Ghirardelli Square, both in San Francisco, might not have been undertaken.

After the first world war, preservation in the United States, as in Europe, became involved with city planning and later with urban renewal. Charleston established the first historic district in the country between 1924 and 1931, New Orleans protected the Vieux Carré in 1936, and many cities followed by establishing historic districts or control through zoning. This practice prevailed in cities that felt themselves to possess, or wished to foster, a distinctive architectural style; and in many cases the zoning laws not only protected old buildings but prescribed the styles of new ones, even in new subdivisions of no particular historical interest:

> Coral Gables, Florida, a town developed during the speculative boom of the 1920's . . . calls for buildings of "Colonial Spanish, Venetian, Italian or other Mediterranean" type . . . while Tombstone, Arizona, limits its designers to "the style and architecture prevalent around Tombstone, Arizona, in the 1880's." Charlottesville, Virginia, will accept Early Virginia, Greek Revival, Mid-Nineteenth Century Vernacular or "contemporary interpretations" of any of these. Santa Fe, New Mexico, has attempted to distinguish between "Old" Pueblo, Pueblo-Spanish, Spanish-Indian, and Territorial flavors.[39]

With respect to urban renewal, there are at present provisions for renewal through restoration of existing structures instead of through clearance, a significant broadening of former renewal schemes, which entailed the preservation of a few old buildings. This program is a response to the criticism by minority groups, preservationists, and social scientists of housing demolition and clearance.

Since the 1930s the federal government has taken several steps to encourage historic preservation. In 1933 the National Park Service began the Historic American Building Survey, a cooperative effort with the Library of Congress and the American Institute of Architects to document buildings of historic and architectural merit. Under the Historic Sites Act of 1935, the park service also started a National Register of Historic Places, which initially included historic areas in the national park system and national historic landmarks. The government also assisted in the restoration of historic landmarks through the Civilian Conservation Corps. It was in this way that the ruin of Mission La Purisima in California was restored between 1934 and 1941.

After World War II American preservationists organized the National Council for Historic Sites and Buildings, which became the National Trust for Historic Preservation with a charter from the

Congress in 1949. This organization acts as a national clearinghouse for preservation matters, publishes a monthly newsletter and a quarterly journal, provides legal advice to other preservation groups, holds seminars and conferences, owns and preserves several historic buildings, and sponsors meetings, tours and other events for those interested in preservation. The trust headquarters are in Washington, and recently it has established regional field offices to provide services in support of regional and local preservation efforts. The trust receives funds both from the federal government and from private sources.

In 1966, with encouragement from the national trust and other groups, the federal government passed a comprehensive Historic Preservation Act that broadened and strengthened federal preservation programs. The act created an Advisory Council for Historic Preservation to advise the president and the Congress and to review the impact of federal agencies' actions and federally financed programs on landmarks listed in the National Register of Historic Places. At the same time, the register began to add state and local historic landmarks through nomination by the states and approval by the register. The act also required the states to designate a State Historic Preservation Office and to undertake a preservation program.

After the Historic Preservation Act, federal involvement with preservation expanded rapidly. In its first seven years, the advisory council reviewed over 400 cases. Although most of these were settled through consultation and negotiation with the agency or program administrators involved in the case, a few critical cases received the attention, study, and recommendation of the entire council. Periodically, the council has published both compliance reports and special reports; the former detail the actions of the council, and the latter relate information on subjects of interest to preservationists. Recent special reports have dealt with local preservation programs, preservation legislation in the Congress, and programs for neighborhood conservation. The council has also formulated guidelines for state historic preservation legislation and has produced lengthy studies of critical cases such as the Old Post Office Building and the Federal Home Loan Bank Board Building, both in the Capital. In these studies the council has documented the historic and architectural significance of the buildings and suggested new adaptive uses for them.

Since 1971, Executive Order 11593 has required all federal agencies to consider the impact of their programs on properties listed in the national register. The Surplus Property Act of 1972 reinforced the federal commitment to preservation by requiring the General Services Administration, which manages government buildings, to consider adaptive reuse for surplus buildings. However, the federal commitment has not been accompanied by adequate funding, and neither the national register nor the advisory council has sufficient staff to process the increasing volume of register nominations and review cases presented to them.

While federal involvement in preservation has increased dramatically, a similar expansion of activities has occurred in the National Trust for Historic Preservation. The trust has begun an extensive publications program, the Preservation Press, that publishes material ranging from books to case studies and reports on specific projects or conferences. In 1971 it created a National Historic Preservation Fund that was to be used as a revolving fund and for a program of preservation grants. In the recently initiated field offices, the trust has attempted to become more directly involved in preservation work and to advise on specific projects and funding available through federal programs. The Boston Regional Office, for example, was established in partnership with the Society for the Preservation of New England Antiquities. Primarily known for its work in preserving colonial houses, the SPNEA has embarked on a more modern program of providing assistance and information on the practical aspects of preservation and restoration. The National Trust Regional Office is part of this program.

The expansion of the trust's involvement in preservation work has been supported by both the Department of Housing and Urban Development and the National Endowment for the Arts. Through grants and matching funds, the trust and local organizations have been able to carry out a number of restoration projects, to start revolving funds, to study proposed projects, and to formulate preservation plans. In this work, the role of the trust is mainly advisory, with the local organizations responsible for actual projects or plans.

The rapid development of the legal and financial framework for preservation in the last decade and the increased federal participation have changed the process of preservation. Nevertheless preservation organizations continue to carry the brunt of preservation work at the municipal level.

Appendix: Criteria for Evaluating Monuments*

A. National significance is ascribed to buildings, sites, objects, or districts which possess exceptional value or quality in illustrating or interpreting the historical (history and archeology) heritage of our Nation, such as:

1. Structures or sites at which events occurred that have made significant contribution to, and are identified prominently with, or which outstandingly represent, the broad cultural, political, economic, military, or social history of the Nation, and from which an understanding and appreciation of the larger patterns of our American heritage may be gained.

2. Structures or sites associated importantly with the lives of persons nationally significant in the history of the United States.

3. Structures or sites associated significantly with an important event that outstandingly represents some great idea or ideal of the American people.

4. Structures that embody the distinguishing characteristics of an architectural type specimen, exceptionally valuable for a study of a period, style, or method of construction; or a notable structure representing the work of a master builder, designer, or architect.

5. Objects that figured prominently in nationally significant events; or that were prominently associated with nationally significant persons; or that outstandingly represent some great idea or ideal of the American people; or that embody distinguishing characteristics of a type specimen, exceptionally valuable for a study of period, style, or method of construction; or that are notable as representations of the work of master workers or designers.

6. Archeological sites that have produced information of a major scientific importance by revealing new cultures, or by shedding light upon periods of occupation over large areas of the

*Source: *Criteria of National Significance,* U.S. Department of Interior, National Register of Historic Places, The National Historic Landmarks Program.

United States. Such sites are those which have produced, or which may reasonably be expected to produce, data affecting theories, concepts, and ideas to a major degree.

7. When preserved or restored as integral parts of the environment, historic buildings not sufficiently significant individually by reason of historical association or architectural merit to warrant recognition may collectively compose a "historic district" that is of historical significance to the Nation in commemorating or illustrating a way of life in its developing culture.

B. To possess national significance, a historic or prehistoric structure, district, site, or object must possess integrity. For an historic or prehistoric site, integrity requires original location and intangible elements of feeling and association. The site of a structure no longer standing may possess national significance if the person or event associated with it was of transcendent importance in the Nation's history and the association consequential.

For a historic or prehistoric structure, integrity is a composite quality derived from original workmanship, original location, and intangible elements of feeling and association. A structure no longer on the original site may possess national significance if the person or event associated with it was of transcendent importance in the Nation's history and the association consequential.

For a historic district, integrity is a composite quality derived from original workmanship, original location, and intangible elements of feeling and association. A structure no longer on the original site may possess national significance if the person or event associated with it was of transcendent importance in the Nation's history and the association consequential.

For a historic district, integrity is a composite quality derived from original workmanship, original location, and intangible elements of feeling and association inherent in an ensemble of historic buildings having visual architectural unity.

For a historic object, integrity requires basic original workmanship.

C. Structures or sites which are primarily of significance in the field of religion or to religious bodies but are not of national importance in other fields of the history of the United States, such as political, military, or architectural history, will not be eligible for consideration.

D. Birthplaces, graves, burials, and cemeteries, as a general rule, are not eligible for consideration and recognition except in cases of historical figures of transcendent importance. Historic sites associated with the actual careers and contributions of outstanding historical personages usually are more important than their birthplaces and burial places.

E. Structures, sites, and objects achieving historical importance within the past 50 years will not as a general rule be considered unless associated with persons or events of transcendent significance.

2. HISTORIC HOUSE MUSEUMS AND HISTORIC DISTRICTS:
The Background of Modern Preservation

We have seen that many of the ideas and tools of preservation were creations of the nineteenth century. Contemporary preservation has continued to add to these. It has developed historic districts, revolving funds, adaptive reuse, and tax incentives for preservation. At the same time, some of the earlier forms of preservation such as museum villages and historic house museums have become less important. These developments are indications of the changing role of preservation in our cities and the gradual emergence of preservation planning in the last three decades.

Prior to the Second World War, the context and rationale of preservation activity was rather different than it is today. Nevertheless, many of the architectural and social elements that made for successful preservation in that time continue to operate in the present. In the nineteenth century, the motive for preservation was predominantly historical, and the resultant activity primarily concerned with monumental buildings. Though we sometimes neglect this fact, the clearly historic or monumental building continues to attract and hold the attention of the public. In this case, preservation often takes the form of an historic house museum.

Historic House Museums

Historic house museums frequently began when an old and historic house received the attention of a group of concerned citizens who sought the public or private purchase of the property for its protection. This practice had become so established by the 1930s that Laurence Coleman, director of the American Association of

Museums, was able to devote a book to the subject—a valuable record that in many ways indicates the high-water mark of this approach. Coleman began with the theme of historic houses, emphasizing the need to preserve colonial and "preindustrial" houses and buildings; went on to discuss the methods and problems of owning and operating a house museum; and finally looked into the prospects for the house museum, proposing the development of museum resorts.

What types of houses were suitable for historic house museums? Today we think first of distinctive architecture, but that is a recent habit. Although architecture was not ignored, it was placed alongside age and historical interest. More importantly, perhaps, what kinds of buildings were likely to survive to become house museums? Here, as Coleman noted, historicity was critical:

> No doubt all but public buildings would soon be doomed were it not for the fact that fate keeps putting the mark of reprieve upon a house here and a house there. Where celebrity is born, where fame makes its home, where art or science labors in erstwhile obscurity, where important incidents occur, where death visits the great—such, for the most part, are the places chosen to survive.[1]

In a contemporary light, this description of buildings likely to survive may seem narrow. However, in its time it characterized the arena of preservation activity, a limited arena for which the house museum was an appropriate technique.

What groups were likely to participate in the establishment of an historic house museum? Coleman suggested a variety of possibilities: "National, state, and local government, patriotic and historical societies, museums, commissions and boards of trustees, and—not least—individuals. Historic houses have brought out a new duty of the state; they have created a new branch of museum work; they have inspired citizens, in groups and individually, to perform useful acts of conservation."[2] The vogue of historic houses from the turn of the century to the depression can be traced to several sources—patriotic sentiments and interest in remnants of the colonial era, the rapid growth of automobile touring, and the popularity of amateur photography. These interests and pursuits motivated the groups

FIGURE 2.1 Juliette Gordon Low House Museum, Girl Scouts of America Southern Regional Headquarters, Savannah

seeking to preserve historic houses. At times, however, this vogue for historic houses led to the excesses of house and room collecting. Museums would purchase historic rooms for removal, reassembly, and display as part of their American collection; naturally these were excellent sets for the display of museum antiques and paintings of the appropriate period, and in the case of a threatened house this practice might be the only way of preserving something. Unfortunately this removal was also done when a house was not threatened with destruction. The collection of entire buildings and their removal to a museum village setting was a rarer practice, as the expense was prohibitive and could only be borne by the very wealthy; it is to this that we owe Henry Ford's Greenfield Village. The goals and functions of Scandinavian museum villages, encouraging craft traditions and craft work, were only vaguely active, if at all, in American museum villages. Mrs. Webb's Shelburne Museum, founded in 1946, is a case in point:

> Just as her collection began with dolls and went on to encompass many
> specialties, her museum began with one building and went on to
> encompass many period structures, all brimming with priceless
> objects. The original building, now known as the Variety Unit, was
> restored and redecorated to house her collection of pewter, ceramics,
> glass, dolls and doll houses. The Horseshoe Barn, built from hand-
> hewn timbers some 60 feet long and taken from 11 old barns in the
> area, contains a collection of more than 200 carriages, sleighs and
> coaches.[3]

Williamsburg, Virginia, restored and recreated by the Rockefeller
family, was also conceived originally as a museum village. On the
whole, contemporary preservationists find the isolation and artificial
atmosphere of the museum village to be foreign to the goals of
current preservation efforts. Walter Muir Whitehill has stated the
objection succinctly:

> Only incidentally do such villages serve the cause of historic
> preservation, for, although they have doubtless rescued from destruc-
> tion some buildings by moving [them], their primary purpose is the
> creation of a well-walled illusion, within which the visitor may enjoy
> a synthetic "past," that relieves the ugliness and monotony of the
> tedium in which he spends most of his life.[4]

The goal of the isolated house museum as well was often the creation
of just such a "well-walled illusion" of the past, at best in its original
setting.

In order to ensure public interest and attraction, Coleman
proposed a series of arrangements for the house museum. A portion of
the house, or preferably the entire house, was to be furnished
according to its historic period as if it were lived in, thus creating a
tableau of the past. Minute details, such as clothes hanging in closets
and letters on tables, were to be arranged so as to provide an air of
authenticity and to create the feeling that the residents had just
stepped out. Museum formality, with explanatory tags and roped off
areas, was to be avoided. A guide was to take the visitor through the
house, providing the missing information through a familiar and
often conjectural talk—thus adding to the informality of the visit.

Questions were invited and the guide could also watch to see that nothing was broken. Anyone visiting a house museum in recent years will recognize the large extent to which Coleman's description still applies.

In another portion of the house, or in a separate building altogether, an appropriate supplementary collection would be on display in a museum arrangement, protected in museum cases and labeled. This part of the historic house might also include a library for research purposes. A third section might be set aside for appropriate souvenirs, postcards, and books about the house; and there could also be an area, of appropriate decor, for refreshments (Coleman recommended tea) and reflection on the experience of the visit. A final portion of the museum should house the administrative and maintenance areas, which would not be usually shown to the public. Again, these arrangements should be familiar to anyone who has recently visited a house museum.

The arrangement of the house museum environment should extend beyond the house also. Coleman recommended the placement of historic markers on the roadside to capture the attention of the passing motor tourist. The grounds should be cultivated to display an appropriate period garden and the outbuildings and servants' quarters restored to reveal typical uses and living arrangements. If the historic house museum was particularly large, it might be necessary to provide a tourist information center and a self-guided brochure for touring the grounds. However, the house tour itself should be conducted by a guide.

Mount Vernon, the progenitor of the historic house museum, displays this arrangement to perfection. Parking, refreshments, and souvenirs are located outside the main gate of the grounds. After paying a nominal fee, to support the preservation work of the Mount Vernon Ladies' Association (MVLA), the visitor enters the grounds and is provided with a brochure—a lengthier book description is also available. On his own, the visitor wanders, perhaps a bit lost, through the large parklike grounds in the direction of the house. Once the house is glimpsed through the trees, the visitor experiences a sense of reassurance and orientation; he rushes forward to it. Unfortunately, as a result of the large number of fellow visitors, especially during the summer, there is a long wait for the guided tour of the house. Some choose to wait, others turn aside to explore the grounds and outbuildings. The work of the MVLA has been thorough and exhaustive. In touring the grounds, the visitor can become familiar with the arrangements of a splendid Virginia plantation after the Revolution. The interior of the kitchens, stables, servant's quarters, and other outbuildings can be viewed, usually from behind a barrier at their doors. The kitchen and gardens have been restored to period; and some of the outbuildings are devoted to museum displays of Washingtoniana.

The interior of Mount Vernon has been restored to its original appearance. After a wait, the visitor follows others in a line through the house and hears the story from the guide. The large number of people visiting Mount Vernon has forced the adoption of this restricted tour that detracts from the usual intimacy that can be achieved in visiting other historic houses. Curiously while most of the grounds are crowded, and the line waiting to enter stretches far away from the house, the lawn reaching down to the Potomac is deserted— for a moment one may actually slip into historic reverie, undisturbed by others. Turning back to the house, the visitor may have the unusual experience of looking in a ground floor window to see a chain of people following one another along a pathway through an historic room. The impression is both disconcerting and unforgettable.

At the conclusion of his book Coleman looked forward to the creation of historic house museum resorts, combining motor tourist camps with historic house museums, where tourists could visit and spend a vacation in historic reflection and leisure. Although Mount Vernon has not taken this step to becoming an historic resort, Williamsburg certainly has. The visitor to Williamsburg has a choice of several accommodations for his stay; once established he confronts a formidable array of sights, daily events, shops, and places to dine.

Williamsburg attracts 20 million visitors annually. It is the most important element in Virginia's Historic Triangle area, which includes Jamestown, Yorktown, and other points of interest along the James River. This formation of a chain of historic house museums was recommended by Coleman, and if Williamsburg is taken as an example, it has become a reality. The attractiveness of this area as a travel destination has been further enhanced for the public by the recent addition of the Old Country–Busch Gardens development adjacent to Williamsburg. As a travel brochure puts it, "The best of

Europe is just five minutes from Williamsburg, Va." The Old Country includes representative reconstructions from England, Scotland, France, and Germany—and partakes of historic simulation as do Disneyland and Knott's Berry Farm in Southern California.

Williamsburg's tourist enterprise, which attempts to provide a more authentic form of the past than Busch's Old Country, is not without problems. Forty percent of Williamsburg visitors as of 1972 used the facility, which is not enclosed by a fence, but did not contribute financial support to the Colonial Williamsburg Foundation. The various programs of the foundation—preservation of buildings and town plan, crafts, interpretation and events, furniture and furnishings, gardens and greens, and preservation research—must be sustained out of admissions and endowment; and this in recent years has not been sufficient. The foundation has attempted to reorganize admissions in order to ensure that more visitors contribute financial support for its programs; however, further measures may be needed in the future. Threatened by its own success, Williamsburg confronts maintenance, program, and security costs that may force it to adopt some of the policies of its commercial rivals.

Most historic house museums have not become historic resorts similar to Williamsburg. This is perhaps fortunate. The appreciation of the historic past and the natural environment is often dependent upon a feeling or illusion of quiet and solitude—even though one may be in a small group of visitors. The illusion quickly fades in the crowds that have become a problem for popular historic areas as well as for the popular national parks.

To relieve this difficulty modern preservationists recognize that the past cannot be isolated in a house museum or museum resort, but should be integrated into the everyday world of our towns and cities. Similarly modern conservationists place nature reserves in the framework of the larger environment, rather than isolating the reserve while the larger environment deteriorates.

The historic house museum and the museum village have their place in contemporary preservation, reconstructing the past of the exceptional building and person. They provide for a concentrated entry into an historic era, for a view of interiors and furnishings, life-styles and crafts that would otherwise not be available. But now we recognize that this is not sufficient, that we must carry preservation into less extraordinary settings where perhaps only an historic exterior is seen, in order to bring historical continuity, perspective, and ambience into our daily lives.

Historic Districts

If the historic house museum and the museum village reflect a method of preservation inherited from the nineteenth century, the development of the historic district marks the beginning of a more comprehensive method of preservation preponderant today. The exact point of origin of the proposal for an historic district is unclear. G. Baldwin Brown's survey of European preservation, published in 1905, makes no reference to historic districts; the focus of concern is rather with isolated monuments. The American Antiquities Act of 1906 is also concerned with isolated buildings and archeological sites; however, the establishment of national parks and monuments on a large scale after the 1870s, under the auspices of the National Park Service, did establish an American precedent for protecting a significant natural or archeological site and its surroundings.

In the 1920s, if not earlier, a new reason for preservation emerged that extended the scope of concern from the single building to the historic district—a growing interest in romantic settings and their ambience. The romantic attitude had influenced the first concern for Gothic buildings in the nineteenth century and had related architectural revivals to restoration. In the 1920s we find a later expression of this relationship in the espousal of architectural control for certain historic areas, namely areas of romantic ambience. This control was to be achieved through the protection of existing buildings and the use of appropriate architectural styles for new structures—thus the historic district was envisioned. Although the first district was not legally recognized until the 1930s, the need to protect historic areas from the encroachment of new buildings that would adversely affect the ambience was felt earlier. Furthermore, it was this romantic ambience that inspired and sustained the first historic districts and that continues to attract today's tourists to these famous areas.

Old and Historic Charleston District

The first historic districts were initiated in Charleston, South

Carolina, by a city zoning ordinance dating from 1931 and in New Orleans, Louisiana, by a state constitutional amendment dating from 1936. In Charleston, the inspiration for this ordinance resulted from a tourist boom and the activities of house collectors:

> In the Boom Days, the town found it had to protect itself from collectors of everything from ironwork to complete houses. Some of these last were taken down and carried off completely, from the brickwork of the basement to the timber of the roof. To guard against such depredations by voicing public opinion, the Society for the Preservation of Old Dwellings was organized and began its invaluable work.[5]

Founded in 1920, the society's first action was the preservation of the Heyworth House, given to the Charleston Museum as an historic house museum in 1929. This was followed by the preparation and passage of a zoning ordinance to protect an "Old and Historic Charleston District." As the first historic district zoning ordinance, which has influenced succeeding laws and ordinances, its provisions deserve consideration.

The Old and Historic Charleston District was established as part of the overall planning and zoning ordinance of 1931. In purpose the historic district was intended to preserve

> the qualities relating to the history of the City of Charleston and a *(ordinance)* harmonious outward appearance of structure which preserve property values and attract tourists and residents alike . . . these qualities being the continued existence and preservation of historic areas and buildings; continued construction of buildings in the historic styles and a general harmony as to style, form, color, proportion, texture, and material between buildings of historic design and those of more modern design.[6]

This was to be achieved through "the preservation and protection of the old historic or architecturally worthy structures and quaint neighborhoods which impart a distinct aspect to the City."[7] The relevant neighborhoods were delineated on the zone maps, and their protection was entrusted to a Board of Architectural Review created by the ordinance.

Although interiors of structures and normal maintenance were excluded from its control, the board had the power to review any erection, demolition, or removal of structures in the historic district, and any changes in "architectural character, general composition and general arrangement of the exterior of a structure, including the kind, color and texture of the building material and type and character of all windows, doors, light fixtures, signs and appurtenant elements, visible from a street or public thoroughfare."[8] Any alteration, construction, or demolition required an application for a certificate of appropriateness. The application procedure consisted of two stages. First, there was an informal review meeting between the applicant and the board to acquaint the applicant with the design standards of the historic district. Preliminary drawings and documents could be considered at this meeting, and in the case of minor projects, the certificate of appropriateness could be approved at this point. For larger projects, a formal application was required. The application had to include relevant architectural plans, such as working drawings, contractors' estimates, and photographs; and the board kept on file suitable examples of architecture, signs, modifications, etc., in order to provide the applicant with suitable or previously approved examples. Once an application was filed, the board had to approve or reject it; in the case of a demolition application, a public hearing was required.

Since the passage of the ordinance, the historic district has been enlarged twice, once in 1966 and again in 1975. In addition, the basic execution of the historic district zoning apparatus has been strengthened by the board's increased authority to delay or prohibit demolitions, to impose penalties to prevent demolition by neglect, and to protect any building older than 100 years in the "Old City" area beyond the historic district proper.

In 1940-1941 the Carolina Art Association, on the recommendation of Frederick Law Olmsted, Jr., undertook a survey of the historic architecture of the city. This was published in 1944 and subsequently revised. Although not part of the zoning ordinance, this survey remained a basic resource for the preservation groups in the city and was only surpassed in 1974 by the inventory that was part of a comprehensive historic district plan prepared for the city.

Historic district zoning has been successful in Charleston. Its shortcomings, which will be taken up later in a discussion of the comprehensive plan of 1974, are matters of degree and scope, reflecting the increasing sophistication of city planning. More pertinent to our immediate concerns is the success of preservation in Charleston—to what factors can it be traced and can we make generalizations from them that will apply to other cities?

Any visitor to the Old and Historic Charleston District will be impressed by the extent of preservation and by its quality. In comparison with many other American cities, the architectural prospect is truly striking. Can the preservationist hope for as much in his own city? It is doubtful—for several reasons. To begin with, Charleston started its preservation effort with a unique architectural and historical heritage. Simply put, there was a great deal to work with. It is not difficult today to distinguish a Charleston style of architecture, replete with Charleston furnishings and decor:

> Though many Charleston houses . . . front the street with doorways flanked by pilasters and topped with fanlights in the Georgian style, the typical Charleston dwelling shows a definite West Indies influence. It turns its narrow side, or shoulder, often only one room wide, to the street. A long pillard piazza, two or three stories tall, faces south onto a side garden secluded behind high walls. Breezes circulate freely through north windows to the piazza, an ideal arrangement in this semitropical climate. The sheltered porch becomes a cool setting for relaxation, and during summer days so much activity is centered here that Charlestonians have cultivated what is known as "northside manners." One does not peer out of one's north windows into the neighbor's south-facing piazza and garden.[9]

Historically, this was the city of John Calhoun, of the firing on Fort Sumter that began the Civil War, of the gracious hospitality and atmosphere of the antebellum South. A second factor, one often neglected in preservation literature, is the relatively small size of the city. In 1970 the population was only 67,000; in 1931 it was smaller. Also the cultural, ethnic, and racial structure of the city is well established and changes slowly. This is a tremendous advantage for preservationists as the cultural elite sensitive to preservation issues are acquaintances if not friends. In a small city the overlap from museum trustees to college board to arts association to Historic Charleston Foundation is likely to be significant. Furthermore, these groups are less subject to cross pressures from conflicting groups and interests that characterize larger and more diverse cities. Therefore, one must be careful in assuming that the Charleston preservation experience can be applied in New York or Chicago.

A third factor in Charleston's history, and one present in the history of other cities that turned to preservation in this period, was the development of a small literary circle (art colonies in other cities) that focused on and elaborated themes and stories of local color and regional character. Led by three men, John Bennet, Harvey Allen, and DuBose Heyward, the Poetry Society of South Carolina was organized in 1920. This society participated in the Southern Literary Renaissance of the 1920s and brought many critics and poets to speak in Charleston.

For preservationists in Charleston, the writing of DuBose Heyward, author of *Porgy,* is best known for its attention to local settings that contributed to the preservation of Church Street.: "In the 1920's the Heyward-Washington House was a bakery, its next neighbor housed Porgy, his goat and his rowdy, exuberant companions. On the other side lived the laundress and her brood. Across the street the elegant Thomas Legare house was in six seedy apartments, its piazzas completely enclosed."[10] In Charleston, the attention to local color in literature was an added help, but was not a factor critical to preservation. The stability of the local society and its interest in its past were far more important and would probably have been sufficient to support preservation. In other cities, this literary or artistic element has played a greater role in encouraging the public's sensitivity to local color and tradition.

The unusual architectural and historical heritage of Charleston, the traditional unity of the local society, and the literary attention to local ambience—all of these factors contributed to the interest in preservation and made the adoption of the Old and Historic District zoning provisions both possible and effective. The factors that made the historic district in Charleston effective have, as we shall see, also been present in other successful instances. Correspondingly, the lack of these or similar elements may be detrimental for an historic district and should be considered in the planning of a proposed district. Further, should one or another element be absent, one should consider if it will be possible to remedy this. Old buildings of interesting architecture alone may not be enough.

Vieux Carré Historic District

The second historic district established in the United States was

FIGURE 2.2 (*above*) Charleston streetscape—Thomas Legare House, St. Philip's Rectory; (*below*) Broad Street commercial buildings, Charleston

intended to protect and preserve the Vieux Carré in New Orleans. The Vieux Carré shared most of the advantages present in Charleston, but as the area is located in the midst of a large city, it has been subject to strong conflicting pressures. The first attempt to protect the Vieux Carré was through passage of a city ordinance in 1924, but this was not enforced. In 1936, an amendment was added by a state referendum to the Louisiana constitution empowering the city of New Orleans to establish an historic district and commission to protect the area. This was carried out by the city in 1937. The use of an amendment to the state constitution to establish an historic district at the local level is an unusual procedure that has not been followed in other cities; it reflects both the difficulty of achieving local control as a result of conflicting development interest and also the statewide concern for this historic area. In recent years the legal position of the Vieux Carré Commission has been stronger than most historic district commissions as a result of this state amendment, but at first it was not so.

The state amendment describes the composition of the commission:

> The members of said Commission shall be appointed by the Mayor as follows: One from a list of two persons recommended by the Curators of the Louisiana State Museum; one from a list of two persons recommended by the Association of Commerce of the City of New Orleans; three qualified architects from a list of six qualified architects recommended by the New Orleans Chapter of the American Institute of Architects; and three to be appointed at large.[11]

The area to be included is also described: "The Vieux Carré Section of the City of New Orleans is hereby defined to comprise all that area within the City limits of the City of New Orleans contained within the following boundaries: The River, Uptown side of Esplanade Avenue, the River side of Rampart Street, and the lower side of Iberville Street."[12] It includes 260 acres and over 3,000 structures. The commission is to preserve the architectural and historical value of the Vieux Carré, using such powers as the New Orleans City Council deems necessary.

The controls applied by the Vieux Carré Commission extend to all exterior work in the quarter:

The exterior of a building is very broadly defined; it includes all elements exposed to the weather, e.g., front, side, and back walls, patio, gallery, balcony, roof, fence, signs, exterior stairs, the sidewalk. Examples of work requiring permits range from the obvious—painting, repairing the facade, remodeling, demolition—to the less obvious—planting trees in the sidewalk, adding an air conditioner tower, replacing shutters, removing stucco over brick, all patio work, signs.[13]

Application procedures and permits are similar to those described for Charleston: major work applications are referred to the Architectural Committee for thorough consideration of plans and may entail several reviews and inspections of work in progress; minor work permits are handled on a routine basis.

The *tout ensemble* concept that plays an important part in planning for the Vieux Carré district was not defined in the initial legislation, but was added in a Supreme Court response decision to a challenge to the Vieux Carré law in 1941: "The purpose of the ordinance is not only to preserve the old buildings themselves, but to preserve the antiquity of the whole French and Spanish quarter, the *tout ensemble*, so to speak, by defending this relic against iconoclasm and vandalism."[14] Through this concept, the commission has been able to extend its control to the minor aspects of the Vieux Carré cityscape, which, while individually not significant, are critical as backdrop and detail for the major elements of the Vieux Carré.

The efforts of the Vieux Carré Commission to preserve the French Quarter have not always met with success. In 1946 the New Orleans City Council excluded certain commercial portions of the Vieux Carré from the control of the commission. These were not returned to its jurisdiction for eighteen years until the action of the city was found to be unconstitutional. During that interval, those portions of the Vieux Carré took on a contemporary commercial character, and this has not been entirely undone even though the commission has now regained control. Furthermore, even in its successful renovation efforts the commission is controversial. Current refurbishings of the Pontalba Apartments and the French Market have met with opposition from those who feel that they undo the quaintness of these areas and make them too expensive for marginal commercial or civic organizations that have traditionally used them. These issues have arisen, however, in the contemporary context, and we will return to them later.

As in Charleston, the protection of the Vieux Carré must be considered in terms of the elements that encouraged its preservation in the first place. To begin with, we again find a unique combination of history and architecture. The history of New Orleans is well known. Originally the early French and later Spanish inhabitants developed a commercial and military settlement on the delta lands along the Mississippi, which passed into American hands with the Louisiana Purchase. As the Americans came into the city they built a rival quarter, the American city across Canal Street, with a different culture and architecture. The commercial activities of the Americans came to eclipse those of the Creole inhabitants of the old city, and the French Quarter began a gradual decline. In the 1850s, fashionable residence was to be found in the new Garden District on the upriver side of the American city and also in other new mansions built away from the French Quarter for wealthy Creoles. The commercial boom that had characterized the city ended with the Civil War. If not for this, the decline of the French Quarter might have been more precipitous, and more of the unusual architecture might have been lost.

The architecture of the French Quarter shows the influence of French and Spanish styles, with colonial elements from the period prior to the Louisiana Purchase. These are in turn overlaid by later French styles of the nineteenth century, with other elements drawn from the American influence. The typical Vieux Carré building, with courtyard, shutters, iron balconies, dormers, and steep roofline, is in this sense a hybrid building, reflecting a succession of styles, influences, uses, and remodelings to current tastes. There are also exceptional buildings in which the design reflects only a single period in the development of Vieux Carré architecture; and it is these buildings, such as Madame John's Legacy, the Ursaline Convent, the Cabildo and Presbytère, Saint Louis Cathedral, the Grima House, Le Carpentier, Beauregard House, the Pontalba buildings, that are most noted, carefully restored, and documented. It is possible to trace the elements of Vieux Carré architecture to various foreign influences, but the *tout ensemble* is unique to New Orleans and is not to

FIGURE 2.3 *(above)* Jackson Square, St. Louis Cathedral, and the Cabildo; *(below)* Upper Pontalba Building

FIGURE 2.4 Courtyard, Grima House

be found elsewhere. This uniqueness is a support to preservationists in their disputes with conflicting interests, and at the same time it is among the initial causes for preservation of the area.

Although it is easy for us to recognize the unique history and architecture of the Vieux Carré, and to desire to preserve it, this was not the prevalent attitude toward the French Quarter prior to the Civil War, or even in the decades that followed. One seldom seeks to preserve a culture with which one is in conflict or competition, as was the case between Americans and Creoles in the first part of the nineteenth century. It is only when an alien culture begins to disappear, when it is no longer a threat, that efforts are made to resuscitate or appreciate what remains. In New Orleans this began to happen in the 1880s with the writings of George W. Cable, Grace King, and Lafcadio Hearn on the Creoles. These writings established the romance and heroism of the Creole settlement of New Orleans and Louisiana and reflected the exotic interest in the remains of Creole culture. This literary enterprise has since been continued, notably in the works of Lyle Saxon, Frances Parkinson Keyes, Harnett Kane, and Robert Tallant.

The literary interest set the stage for the rehabilitation of the French Quarter, but this did not begin to occur until the period of the First World War and the 1920s with the establishment of an art colony in the Vieux Carré. Lyle Saxon played a central role in this development by renting for sixteen dollars a sixteen-room house on Royal Street where he lived and invited his friends, creating a literary salon. This was a ground breaking effort:

> Leasing that Royal Street house and moving into the French Quarter as it was then was startling, even shocking, to a degree that may seem incomprehensible now. Some old people, descendants of the Creoles, still clung with a kind of grim tenacity to a few of the old homes, but all the other buildings were occupied by the extremely poor, often by criminals. After dusk few respectable persons ventured into the neighborhood. Thugs waited in dark alleyways. Prostitutes stood naked behind shuttered doors and windows. The courtyards, once so beautiful, were often filled with refuse and incredible filth. Saxon was told he would be murdered. Once this almost happened.[15]

Saxon's example and persuasion, abetted by low rents and exotic ambience, led other artists to establish themselves in the quarter.

In the 1920s the art colony became large and well known and numbered William Faulkner and Sherwood Anderson among its residents. Faulkner described the Vieux Carré as it was then:

> Do you know our quarter, with its narrow streets, its old wrought-iron balconies and its southern European atmosphere? An atmosphere of richness and soft laughter, you know. It has a kind of ease, a kind of awareness of the unimportance of things that outlanders like my-self . . . were taught to believe important. So it is no wonder that as one walks about the quarter one sees artists here and there on the shady side of the street corners, sketching houses and balconies. I have counted as many as forty in a single afternoon, and though I did not know their names or the value of their paintings, they were my brothers.[16]

The picturesque atmosphere of the French Quarter provided the material and setting that the artists and writers needed in their work, and even today there are many artists in the quarter who continue in this vein.

As the literati found the quarter amenable to their work, they also came to defend it and to seek its improvement and preservation. In this they made common cause with those groups in New Orleans society that also valued the old French Quarter and sought its preservation. These included the Beauregard Memorial Association (organized to preserve the Beauregard House that the owner had intended to turn into a macaroni factory), the Christian Women's Exchange (owners of the Grima House and Exchange Shop), and the Louisiana State Museum (preserving the Presbytère and the Cabildo). These groups may not have mingled socially, but they shared a common interest in preservation in the Vieux Carré.

In the 1920s the method of preservation was not clearly established, and a romantic treatment, such as Pirate's Alley next to the Cabildo, based more on fantasy than fact was possible. At the same time the opposition to preservation was not clearly developed, especially in an area as stagnant as the Vieux Carré had become. The literary, artistic, and historic sentiments broadcast from the art colony created a receptivity to preservation that crystallized in support for the statewide referendum of 1936. However, only after 1937 did the preservation effort begin in earnest, and only then did opposition begin in earnest. Perhaps because of the size of the city, preservation did not have the same degree of consensual support that was found in Charleston, and this has remained true to the present.

The background of preservation in Charleston and New Orleans shows several elements that contributed to the successful establishment of historic districts—a unique history and architecture, an awareness of this history and architecture encouraged by literature and art, and the support of various groups, or social elite as a whole, for preservation. A fourth element that stimulated preservation sentiments in the 1920s and 1930s, namely architectural revivals, must also be considered in the success of historic districts. This fourth element was not present in Charleston, but there is some evidence that it did play a small part in New Orleans. In 1922 a new theater, Le Petit Theatre, was built in the Vieux Carré by Armstrong and Koch, and this building was done "in the character of the older structures surrounding it."[17] Richard Koch also restored several buildings in the Vieux Carré in this period and later. The Pirate's Alley could also be considered a romantic revival—but aside from these few examples, new buildings in the old styles did not play a significant role in New Orleans.

Preservation and Architectural Revival: Santa Fe and Santa Barbara

The possible role of architectural revival in promoting an historic district can better be illustrated by considering the course of events in Santa Fe, New Mexico, and Santa Barbara, California. In both of these cities during the 1920s and 1930s, a number of new buildings were constructed in Spanish colonial revival styles derived from and thus calling attention to the existing adobe architecture. Furthermore, both cities came to allow only this style and related interpretations in and around the areas that were to become their historic districts after World War II. This dictation of architectural style is too extreme for many contemporary preservationists, yet it has its adherents who argue that it is a more viable way of preserving and continuing the unique architectural tradition of a city.

The course of events in Santa Fe did not at first lead to a focus on historic preservation. The activities of those who sought to maintain and continue the life-style of Old Santa Fe took a number of other forms. The first stage in the recognition, and from that the appreciation, of this life-style was the formation of a self-conscious art colony in the town before and after World War I. Although there were Santa Fe enthusiasts among ethnographers, artists, photographers, and tourists prior to 1910, they had only a minor impact on the life of Santa Fe until the formation of the colony. The events that ensued from the realization of the uniqueness of Old Santa Fe have been recounted in Oliver La Farge's biography of the town. La Farge was himself one of the participants in this transformation that has given us the Santa Fe we know today.

The activities of the art colony began to be visible in 1916 with the exhibition of paintings of the Southwest in the old Palace of the Governors. The demand for exhibition space outran what was available and required the building of an art museum in 1917. The museum was designed by Carlos Vierra and initiated a modern Santa Fe style that imitates adobe architecture:

> Made of cement, hollow tile, and plaster, it attempts unsuccessfully to imitate true adobe . . . the workmen "freed themselves from plumb-line and square," in short, were under orders to lay up the courses out of true, so as to give the effect of adobe after it has settled. The exterior details of the Museum are copied from a number of mission churches, portions of Indian pueblos, and other sources. The total effect is stagey and not particularly interesting; nonetheless, this building was beneficially important in leading to the development of the modern Santa Fe style.[18]

Vierra advocated this style for new buildings in the town and built several cottages in the style himself; other artists followed. In the building boom after 1920 the picturesque Santa Fe style predominated, both in the artist's colony on Canyon Road and Camino del Monte Sol, and in the downtown Plaza area where the La Fonda hotel, the post office, and other buildings were constructed. The La Fonda, built through public subscription in the early 1920s and later operated by the Fred Harvey Hotel chain, was notable as a social center that embodied the new-old image of Santa Fe and conveyed it to both residents and tourists.

Historic preservation in Santa Fe is today associated with the Old Santa Fe Association founded in 1926. However, the association had other purposes, at least at first. The association came into existence during a controversy over a Chautauqua-like culture colony for the

FIGURE 2.5　The Plaza and Palace of the Governors, Santa Fe

Southwestern Federation of Women's Clubs that had been proposed by the chamber of commerce and approved by the city council. The members of the art colony and other residents who wished to protect Santa Fe from an incursion of culture seekers opposed the project and organized the Old Santa Fe Association "for the purpose of working for the preservation of Old Santa Fe, and of guiding new growth and development and advancement in material welfare, in such a way as to sacrifice as little as possible of the unique charm and distinction of this city, born of age, tradition and environment, and which are Santa Fe's most priceless assets."[19] Although the culture colony project faded in the face of outspoken hostility, the Old Santa Fe Association remained to affect the course of change in the city.

After the demise of the culture colony, the Old Santa Fe Association turned its attention to the Santa Fe fiesta, which dated according to legend from the earliest days of the city. The chamber of commerce revived it in 1912, again in 1916, and thereafter as a tourist attraction, an historic pageant with a paid admission. In 1926 the art colony, through the Old Sante Fe Association, staged an open fiesta, called El Pasatiempo, which reestablished the free public fes-

FIGURE 2.6   Santa Fe revival style: *(above)* First phase—Federal Building; *(below)* Current phase—First National Savings and Loan Building

tival and has been continued annually to the present.

The involvement of the Old Santa Fe Association with preservation per se did not occur until the 1950s, and an historic zone with architectural controls was not established until 1957. Since that time the association and a related organization, the Historic Santa Fe Foundation (founded 1961), have taken on a more typical concern with preservation in the city through their ownership of several buildings and involvement in several demolition controversies. Nevertheless, we should note again the role of the artists' colony, the architectural revival, and also the fiesta in creating the preconditions for historic preservation in Santa Fe. Without these kinds of preconditions, preservation moves in a vacuum, and the sympathies of society are likely to be elsewhere. The natural affinities of historic tradition and architecture, art colonization, architectural revival, and civic festivity, are not givens of the social world. Some cities, such as Charleston and New Orleans, are fortunate in their endowments; others, such as Santa Fe, must work to create them.

The history of preservation in Santa Barbara illustrates another such effort at creation. Unlike Santa Fe, the Spanish adobe and mission heritage of Santa Barbara was largely overshadowed by the culture of American settlers until it was consciously revived in the 1920s. Prior to World War I, Spanish cultural themes were not predominant in the civic image or architecture of Santa Barbara. Photographs of public and commercial buildings in the period do not reveal the use of a Spanish revival building style; rather the architecture follows conventional American styles of the time. The first evidence of a revival of Spanish influences on Santa Barbara architecture can be found in the designs of several tourist hotels. The first hotel to use a mission revival style was the Potter, designed by John Austin in 1901 and constructed in 1902. Its luxury and elegance surpassed that of the well-known Arlington, which had been the best hotel in the city. In 1909 the original wood frame building of the Arlington was destroyed by fire, and it was rebuilt in a Spanish style from a design by Arthur Benton that incorporated towers, gables, and cloistered walks reminiscent of the Mission Inn in Riverside. A third hotel, El Mirasol, also made use of the mission style for its main building. However, in the construction of mission revival style hotels, Santa Barbara followed the example set by other cities in

Southern California as well. Thus the revival effort was not yet solely
a response to the heritage of Santa Barbara.

Other evidence of the renewed interest in a Spanish style of
architecture can be seen in three houses built in the Montecito area of
Santa Barbara in 1916 and 1917. The Bliss house of 1916, designed by
Carleton Winslow, exhibited the churrigueresque details that
characterized his work at the San Diego Exposition of 1915. The
Heberton house of 1916, the first house by George Washington Smith
in California, used a Spanish provincial style that Smith and James
Osborne Craig were to develop for Santa Barbara houses after the
war. Finally, the Peabody house of 1917, designed by Francis T.
Underhill, was done in a Mediterranean style. This evidence of a taste
for Spanish architecture among the wealthy of Montecito, and of the
formation of a group of architects to cater to that taste, is significant
in the light of what followed.

The development of the Spanish and Mediterranean revival style in
Santa Barbara was encouraged after the war by the activities of the
Community Arts Association, which advocated Spanish style
architecture, made efforts to preserve old adobes, and organized a
fiesta for the city. Its leader, Bernard Hoffman, settled in the city in
1920 and became active in the association shortly after it was formed.
In 1921 he organized an advisory committee to aid in the planning for
a new city hall and in the renovation of the adjacent de la Guerra
Plaza. Hoffman also became interested in restoring old adobes from
their dilapidated condition. At the time the association was looking
into the possibility of restoring the historic Casa de la Guerra, with a
compatible commercial development: "Mr. and Mrs. Hoffman
purchased Casa de la Guerra—the historic tile-roofed adobe facing
the Plaza and faithfully following the remarkable sketch plans of
James Osborne Craig, successively built around it the famous 'Street
in Spain,' El Restaurante del Paseo . . . , the de la Guerra Studios, the
State Street entrance and the Anacapa wing."[20] When Craig died
unexpectedly in 1922, a memorial exhibition of his sketch-plans was
held, and his designs for El Paseo, as the development around the
adobe was called, were carried out in the following years under the
direction of Carleton Winslow.

In 1923 the Community Arts Association sponsored a general plan
study for the city. Although the plan was not officially adopted, its
argument in favor of Spanish style architecture was felt in the Spanish

FIGURE 2.7 *(above)* El Paseo and Oreña Adobe; *(below)* El Paseo—"Street in Spain"

design of the city hall and the Lobero Theatre by George Washington Smith. The interest of the association in the old adobes led several members each to buy and restore one of the old dwellings. In one case, the Fremont Adobe, which was threatened by construction in 1922, was taken down and reconstructed on another site. By publicizing the community plan, the advantages of Spanish style architecture and adobe preservation, the association prepared the way for a major Spanish style reconstruction of the city after the earthquake of 1925.

The Community Arts Association was also involved in the creation of the Old Spanish Days Fiesta first celebrated in 1924. They modeled the fiesta on certain aspects of prewar celebrations that had included the participation of members of the old Spanish families in traditional costume and the performance of early California dances, the Contradanza and La Jota. In 1920 the city made an effort to establish an annual presentation of historic costumes, dance songs and folklore. A dramatic pageant, "Primavera, the Masque of Santa Barbara," was written and presented in a natural amphitheater. However, despite a good reception, it was not repeated the following year.

The Old Spanish Days Fiesta of 1924 resulted from the wish of the arts association to celebrate the opening of the new Lobero Theatre and the desire of the business community to attract and entertain summer tourists. The two groups formed a committee and planned the fiesta, which included an historical parade, a celebration at the theatre, and aquatic sports events. Material used for the Primavera masque was incorporated into the plan to present the heritage of the city. The fiesta was held for four days in August, and its success led to the formation of a permanent organization to present it annually.

The Spanish revival in Santa Barbara, which the Community Arts Association fostered, was further realized after the destructive earthquake of 1925 damaged a fourteen-block section of the business district along State Street. The identification of Spanish style architecture with the heritage of the city generated renewed commitment in the community to rebuild in this style. Following the earthquake, the city government established a Board of Public Safety and Reconstruction to coordinate emergency programs, and the board appointed an Architectural Advisory Committee, with Bernard Hoffman as chairman, to coordinate the planning and rebuilding with architects and buisnessmen. An advisory board of forty-two prominent citizens helped to secure the cooperation of the business community, and block subcommittees were organized along State Street to facilitate rebuilding of the blocks with harmonious Spanish style facades.

The efforts of the architectural committee were enhanced by the appointment of an Architectural Board of Review by the city council. The board of review was partially able to regulate the rebuilding since without its report on the exterior design of the building, a building permit would not be issued. In order to encourage the use of plans and designs in harmony with the views of the architectural committee and the board of review, a privately sponsored Community Drafting Room was established to provide free plans for the rebuilding and to make changes in plans sent over from the board:

> It prepared suggestions for the harmonious treatment of whole block fronts; for stores, garages and the simpler forms of buildings, to conform to a style considered fitting for the region, yet strictly within the requirements and costs of the owner.
>
> In this manner, numerous buildings of all types were transformed into public and private assets. In several blocks of narrow stores an appearance of "unified architecture" was achieved by using off-white and light earth colors on the walls, and related colors for trim."[21]

In February 1926 the ordinance authorizing the architectural board was revoked, thus effectively ending the regulation of architectural style. Nevertheless, in the eight-month life of the board, the Spanish revival style was firmly established as predominant in Santa Barbara.

The Spanish revival of the 1920s has remained a permanent feature of Santa Barbara culture and cityscape. The fiesta is celebrated annually, and the activities of the Community Arts Association have been continued by the Santa Barbara Historical Society. Most of the historic adobes have been preserved as private residences or for various public uses. An historic district, El Pueblo Viejo, was established in the early 1960s, and the architectural styles permitted for new buildings in the district were restricted to California adobe, early Monterey, Spanish and Spanish colonial, and Mediterranean styles compatible with the neighboring buildings in the district. Decisions on style are made by a new Architectural Board of Review and can be appealed to the city council. As in Santa Fe, the conditions for preservation in Santa Barbara were enriched by the Spanish revival of the 1920s, and the historic cityscape is protected not only through preservation but through the limitation of the styles of new building in the historic district.

Is this ok?

Many different conditions have fostered the development of historic districts: unique historic and architectural traditions, social groups that are conscious of these traditions and seek to enhance them, architectural revivals and related civic festivals. In Charleston and New Orleans these factors were present from the beginning, in Santa Fe and Santa Barbara they had to be fostered. In contemporary preservation other factors, including tourism, neighborhood preservation, and adaptive reuse have become important. Tourism as a goal may support preservation, or it may create a kind of commercialism that is antithetical to the best interest of an historic area. Neighborhood preservation may encourage community involvement, civic festivals and awareness of tradition and architecture, or it may stimulate real estate speculation and chic restorations that can undermine the benefits to the community as a whole. Adaptive reuse may find a new function for an old building that respects its historic identity, or it may destroy that identity through mishandling in the rush to make the building economically viable. These new possibilities reflect contemporary circumstances, but our understanding of them will be more adequate insofar as we have examined the more traditional social functions and affinities of preservation.

3. HISTORIC COMMISSIONS AND HISTORIC DISTRICTS:
Contemporary Practice and Problems

The historic commissions and districts developed for preservation in Charleston and New Orleans set precedents for similar commissions and districts established in other cities after World War II. This approach to preservation has proven successful, but the historic commissions and districts are not without their problems. Some of these problems result from the legal inadequacies of the commissions, others result from the practical details of district preservation and from the pressures on the district from the larger city.

Since World War II, ordinances for the establishment of historic commissions and for the designation of landmarks and historic districts have been adopted in a large number of cities. These municipal efforts have been supported and reinforced by state and federal legislation directed toward similar goals. At the municipal level extremely varied controls and limits have been adopted. The details of various legal approaches can be found in Jacob Morrison's book on historic preservation law.[1] For our purposes, however, it is sufficient to elucidate the strengths and weaknesses of the historical commissions and districts by exploring some contemporary cases.

The success of an historic commission is not entirely a product of its legal powers; politics and community support for preservation are probably as important. Nevertheless, we may ordinarily assume that a commission with limited legal powers will be able to achieve little, while one with broader powers will be able to do more. As a social process, preservation depends upon active preservation groups in the communty, awareness of and surveying of historic areas, publicity about these areas, description of the areas by the historic commission, municipal support, and encouragement of private efforts within the areas. The parts of the process are not independent of each other, and they may not work well alone. For an example of a weak commission and a dispersed preservation process, one may consider the course of preservation in Los Angeles.

Cultural Heritage Board: Los Angeles

Preservation is no stranger to Los Angeles. Efforts to save the historic buildings of El Pueblo de Los Angeles, in the downtown area, can be traced back to the 1920s and continue to the present. The Will Rogers home is preserved as a state historic park, and various adobes around the city have been preserved by private organizations or turned over to the city. The Hollyhock House, designed by Frank Lloyd Wright, is also owned by the city, and its location in Barnsdall Park has, with the addition of several complementary buildings, become the Municipal Art Center. In 1962, a Cultural Heritage Board was established by city ordinance. In recent years, the city has participated in a Heritage Square project on vacant land adjacent to the Pasadena Freeway, and several old buildings threatened with demolition have been moved there. Despite these various evidences of preservation activity, Los Angeles is generally considered to be in the rearguard of preservation.

Several problems confront preservation in Los Angeles that are not common in other cities. Aside from a few adobes, most buildings in Los Angeles are of recent origin, that is, post-Victorian; as a result they are not strikingly historic due to age—as is often true in the older Eastern cities. For the average citizen, the aesthetic of newness and the development syndrome hold sway; real estate speculation has been and continues to be extensive. Furthermore, the sprawling growth of the city and the succession of developed centers ever farther from the downtown area have worked against widespread public sympathy for or knowledge of the historic areas of initial development in and around the downtown. For example, there is no lack of interesting older buildings from the period of the First World War in the areas near downtown, but there is certainly a public ignorance of these distinctive areas of the city. A parallel could easily be drawn between the West Adams area of Los Angeles and the area that became the Swiss Avenue Historic District in Dallas. Both areas date from the same time, and both share a mixture of mansions adjacent to humbler residences.[2] Yet the West Adams neighborhood, now predominantly a black area, has not been proposed as an historic district, nor is this likely to occur. In order to explain this inaction, the institutional and social factors in Los Angeles must be taken into account.

The institutional organization of preservation in Los Angeles centers around the city-administered Cultural Heritage Board, a part of the Municipal Arts Department. Established in 1962, the Cultural Heritage Board has received the support of various local historical societies and women's groups. Its main function has been the designation of historic and cultural monuments worthy of preservation; over 100 of these have been so designated at the suggestion of various groups or individuals. However, the board itself has not undertaken a systematic survey of the historic areas of the city, and its actions in preserving designated buildings have been largely reactive. This is reflected in the policy of moving threatened Victorian buildings to Heritage Square. The first two buildings moved to the square, from the Bunker Hill Urban Renewal Project, were burned to the ground by vandals; however, succeeding buildings moved there have been more fortunate. The Heritage Square project is conducted by the Cultural Heritage Foundation, an offshoot of the Cultural Heritage Board. Since 1969 this time-consuming and costly process of moving a few houses to a freeway-isolated arroyo littoral, in order to establish a Victorian block, has monopolized the energies of preservationists in Los Angeles. In terms of the effort expended, the results have been minimal; and perhaps more significantly, to the public at large they have been almost invisible.

Los Angeles has not been the only city in which old houses have been saved by moving them to a heritage landmark area. In San Francisco, the Foundation for San Francisco's Architectural Heritage saved twelve Victorian houses from the Western Addition Urban Renewal Project by sponsoring their removal to vacant lots in a block adjacent to the project area where there were buildings of similar age and style. The houses are being sold by the Redevelopment Agency to private buyers and will be restored to agency standards. These houses and those already on the block will comprise the Beideman Place Historic Area. The moving of the houses attracted more publicity than similar moves have in Los Angeles, and the Beideman Place area

FIGURE 3.1   (*above* and *below*) Heritage Square, Los Angeles

is a viable setting for the houses. However, much has been lost in the urban renewal clearance, and the moving of the houses to Beideman Place was a measure of last resort to save the most notable Victorians in the clearance area.

Another heritage park is being developed in Denver where Historic Denver, Inc., has saved a block of Victorian houses from clearance as part of the land for the Auraria Higher Education Center. The sixteen houses in the Ninth Street Historic Park are being restored with funds from Historic Denver and from other sponsoring organizations, and some of the restored houses will be put to new uses by the colleges to be built in the Auraria Center. Once again, the clearance for the education center, like other clearance projects in Denver, has destroyed more than preservationists have been able to preserve, and what buildings have been saved are more museum pieces than integral parts of a preservation district. However, Historic Denver has received substantial publicity from its restoration work on Ninth Street and from other organization activities, such as the annual Night in Old Denver celebration, so that it may be more successful in promoting preservation in the future.

For preservation to be most effective, it must capture the

FIGURE 3.2   Ninth Street Historic Park, Denver

imagination of a city; it must appear frequently in the newspapers and magazines; and it must be talked about. This has happened in Seattle, San Francisco, New Orleans, and Savannah and has begun to happen in Denver, but it has not in Los Angeles. This is not due to lack of old buildings—there are enough. Nor is it because Angelenos are uninterested in the past; there are any number of restaurants and shopping centers with nostalgic antique decorations that appeal to similar sentiments. Rather the preservationists in Los Angeles have so far taken an approach to preservation, the designation of single buildings, that does not capture public attention. Part of the difficulty seems to be that the ordinance establishing the Cultural Heritage Board does not provide for historic districts. In one potential historic district area, Carroll Avenue, the board has had to designate the residences on both sides of the avenue individually; this is a cumbersome process. Clearly, the ordinance should be amended to provide for historic districts, and this should be a first priority for preservationists in Los Angeles.

The social difficulties of preservation in Los Angeles go beyond the shortcomings of the Cultural Heritage Board. The areas of greatest potential for preservation, areas like West Adams, or the older sections of Hollywood, are increasingly inhabited by the poorer groups in the city—recent Spanish-speaking immigrants, Koreans and other Asians, and blacks. The younger middle-class couples who support preservation in many other cities have been drawn out to the suburbs or to the west side of the city. As yet there is no "back-to-the-city" movement. However, the shortage of new housing, and its expense, may encourage such a movement, as has occurred recently in other cities. At that point, the social pressure for the designation of historic districts may increase; as of now, it hardly exists.

Another way to overcome the present preservation impasse in Los Angeles might be for the city government to foster preservation among the groups presently living in the historic areas of the city. Recently the city has undertaken a program of providing low-interest loans for rehabilitation of several target neighborhoods around the city. Although this was not placed in the historic preservation context, the response of neighborhood residents in at least one instance revealed commonly held apprehensions toward preservation and rehabilitation in general.

The residents were informed by mail of the program, and a public

FIGURE 3.3   Harvard Boulevard, West Adams area, Los Angeles: *(above)* Rindge House; *(below)* Unrestored house

meeting was held to explain the details. At one meeting the public reaction was one of hostility and suspicion. Why were the loans being made? To put them further in debt? To raise property values and taxes? Thus, to push them out of the area? The issues raised go beyond preservation, and they pose problems preservationists might not anticipate. Yet for preservation to be effective they must be considered.

Many of the poor may suspect that they cannot afford preservation or rehabilitation. Their immediate problems of food, clothing, work, and protection from crime seem to them to go beyond the amenity of neighborhood improvement. They may be mistaken; however, it rests upon preservationists to prove their own case by integrating building restoration with the solution of other problems before the poor will be won over. This may be asking too much of preservation, in which case we must acknowledge that preservation, like the collecting of antiques, is a luxury of those who can afford it. There may be nothing wrong with this, but if it is true it should be acknowledged so as to avoid false expectations. At this point, however, our consideration of the question is only a beginning; we will find out more from other cities.

Philadelphia Historical Commission

While the Los Angeles Cultural Heritage Board has shown us the problems that can result from a weak municipal preservation ordinance, the Philadelphia Historical Commission (PHC) can provide us with a counterpoint. The historical commission was established by city ordinance in 1956 and was the first such commission to be given authority over the entire area of a city, with a mandate to certify historic buildings, to approve appropriate alterations, and to delay demolition. The initial and ongoing task of the commission was the identification and certification of historic buildings. In the process a file was developed on the buildings, and this file was maintained for municipal and public reference. Currently the commission has over 4,000 buildings listed as historic, and the certification process continues. So far, this process is rather similar to what we have just seen in Los Angeles, with the difference that the Philadelphia commission is more actively involved in surveying and listing buildings. Yet if it stopped at that, we might expect preservation in Philadelphia to be ineffective, which it is not. First, the commission must be consulted when alterations are proposed for the exterior of a listed building. Second, and more unusual, the PHC since its inception in 1956 has worked in alliance with the City Planning Commission and the Philadelphia Redevelopment Authority to further preservation in the city. The cooperation is noteworthy, considering that planning and urban renewal during the mid-fifties were often equated with clearance and demolition. It suggests that sensitivity to the city's historical and architectural tradition was as well developed in Philadelphia as we have previously seen in Charleston and New Orleans.

This conclusion is not unwarranted. The preservation movement in Philadelphia can trace its roots back to the restoration of Independence Hall in the last century and more recently to the formation of the Philadelphia Society for the Preservation of Landmarks after World War I. The convergence of city planning and preservation focused initially on the Independence Hall area:

> Planning for the historic old city had begun in 1937 when the committee on Municipal Improvements of the American Institute of Architects proposed a mall north of Independence Hall and a greenway connecting the distinguished buildings to the east of it. In 1944, the Independence Hall Association presented a comprehensive plan based on the 1937 study and suggested rehabilitation of the entire area east of 7th Street from Pine to Race. The proposal included sites for apartments and town houses, and a recreation area along the waterfront.[3]

The Independence Hall Mall Project was carried out with federal assistance after World War II. The restoration of the adjacent Society Hill area, as part of the Washington Square redevelopment area, was overseen by the Phildelphia Redevelopment Authority and the City Planning Commission.

The Washington Square project combined, in an innovative fashion, the processes of urban renewal, new building, and rehabilitation. In this it became an example for other similar projects in other cities, and the basic procedures still continue in use. The Washington Square area included the old Dock Street Markets and the Society Hill area. Once the redevelopment district was authorized, the entire area became subject to the eminent domain powers of the Philadelphia Redevelopment Authority. The Dock Street Markets, a wholesale produce market, was relocated at a new food distribution center in South Philadelphia. The new market provided modern facilities and easy truck transport access, thus increasing the efficiency of its services to the Philadelphia area. Interestingly, this successful market relocation established a precedent followed in other cities, often to the chagrin of preservationists:

> During 1963 and 1964, a steady stream of French architects, city planners, government officials, and private builders and entrepreneurs passed through the Food Distribution Center, asking many questions. After hundreds of years, the famous Paris wholesale food mart, Les Halles, is being closed and moved to an outlying part of the city where the new market patterned after Philadelphia's successful and modern Food Distribution Center is being constructed.[4]

The Dock Street Market buildings were demolished, making way for the development of high-rise apartment towers, designed by I. M. Pei for Alcoa Residences.

At the same time, the Philadelphia Redevelopment Authority approached owners in the Society Hill area and asked them to rehabilitate their buildings, or to sell them to private parties who would rehabilitate or to the authority. The rehabilitation effort of the authority was aided by the Old Philadelphia Development Corporation, a business leaders' group formed in 1956, which screened suitable buyers for properties acquired by the authority. The restoration plans and work were overseen by the authority and the historical commission. Some buildings in the Society Hill area, very deteriorated or architecturally inappropriate, were acquired by the authority and demolished. The land was then sold for residential development with the use of both historic styles and compatible contemporary design allowed.

The Philadelphia Redevelopment Authority described the following ways of buying an historic house:

> Let's say Mr. and Mrs. X wished to buy an historic house and restore it. They can proceed in several ways:
> 1. They can purchase a property from an owner in an urban renewal area, such as Society Hill, who is voluntarily

FIGURE 3.4 (*above* and *below*) Society Hill—contemporary and historic buildings

restoring the house, or who has a rehabilitation contract with
the Redevelopment Authority; or

2. In Society Hill, they were able to buy a house from the
   Redevelopment Authority (through its designated redeveloper, the Old Philadelphia Development Corporation, and be
   selected as OPDC's nominee). They submitted architectural
   plans for rehabilitation and showed proof that they were
   financially able to carry them out.

3. Mr. and Mrs. X may buy an historic house that is not in an
   urban renewal area, in which case they deal only with the
   owner or his agent. If the house is certified, they present their
   renovation plans to the Historical Commission. The Commission also can verify whether a property is certified.[5]

The restoration standards set by the authority and the historical
commission, added to the expense of renovating the interior, made
restoration in Society Hill an expensive, and thus often exclusive,
proposition. This was reflected in the ratio of public to private
investment. "One measure of Society Hill's success is that private
investment—a good yardstick in urban renewal—funds almost
double the national 3 to 1 average . . . That would put the investment
of individuals and developers at $165 million to $180 million. Some
have spent up to $200,000 to restore a house."[6] Land values and
property taxes increased substantially in Society Hill during the
restoration process, and it was transformed from a dilapidated into a
desirable neighborhood.

The cooperation of the City Planning Commission, Philadelphia
Redevelopment Authority, Philadelphia Historical Commission and
Old Philadelphia Development Corporation has continued beyond
the Society Hill project into the current Washington Square West
redevelopment area. The same procedures used in Society Hill have
been applied in this area, but with some noteworthy problems not
encountered in Society Hill. First, the Society Hill restoration was
innovative and thus considered risky. Although speculation occurred
in Society Hill, it was not a major problem. Second, the houses in
Society Hill were relatively small, two and three stories, and could be
restored without major difficulties resulting from size. Third, in the
case of buildings acquired by the authority, the resale price, which
took into account restoration cost and was therefore sold at a loss to
the authority, was sufficiently low to attract private buyers.

FIGURE 3.5 Washington Square West

In the Washington Square West redevelopment area the conditions have been different. Because preservation proved a success in Society Hill, speculation drove up the price of properties in the adjacent Washington Square West area. This effectively limited private restoration efforts, and at the same time, raised the price that the Philadelphia Redevelopment Authority had to pay when it condemned property. The houses in Washington Square West, built at a later and more prosperous time than those in Society Hill, are larger, often four stories. This makes renovation more expensive and poses further problems in their maintenance and heating. Finally, as a result of the higher prices paid by the authority, the resale price, though below market value, is still so high that, when restoration costs are figured in, the private buyer is faced with a considerable investment. For these reasons, the restoration of Washington Square West has proceeded at a much slower pace than that of Society Hill.

These considerations may seem unduly technical, but they bring to light certain problems that confront preservationists throughout the country. The restoration of private residences is a costly and time-consuming exercise, as well as a labor of love; it is also an investment in many cases. If, as in Society Hill, the properties are reasonably priced, indeed bargains, then there seem to be enough people committed to preservation to make a success of the rehabilitation effort with municipal backing, and also often at first without that backing. But the very success of preservation attracts speculators who seek a quick profit by driving up the price and selling the property without any renovation. This makes preservation a less attractive investment and disheartens the serious preservationist. In the end the speculators may stymie the entire preservation process.

One solution has been to purchase properties quietly, using group resources, and to resell them to interested preservationists with convenants requiring restoration by the purchaser within a certain period of time. This same policy was used by the Philadelphia Redevelopment Authority, which required that purchasers of its properties carry out restoration. However, in both of these cases only a few properties are affected, and the majority are still subject to the speculation that ensues once the publicity for preservation has begun to have an effect.

The successful restoration of Society Hill was one of the first large-scale municipally supported efforts; as such it has received its share of criticism. Society Hill has become a symbol of the potential elitism of preservation. Whatever the former social character of the area, today it is almost exclusively upper middle class in composition. The environment of Society Hill is uniformly neat and clean, well-ordered and some would say, sterile; in this, the former social ambience is gone. One can hardly even guess what it was. The area of the historic Second Street Market is surrounded by shops for tourists, and the market itself is given over to handicraft vendors. As a whole, Society Hill is rather like the museum villages described earlier by W. M. Whitehall; it is history in a showcase. This is not to say that the quiet and serenity of Society Hill do not have a place in preservation, but that the addition of some of the vitality and interest of varied human enterprises, such as can still be seen in the Italian market of South Philadelphia, or no doubt could have been found in the demolished, rat-infested old Dock Street Markets, also has its place in preservation. The preservation of Pike's Place Market in Seattle and efforts to save old markets and find adaptive uses for them in other cities reflect a new recognition of the need for diverse milieux and their respective activities. If the restoration of Society Hill had occurred more recently, the Dock Street Markets might have been included in the restoration process.

Furthermore, the cooperation between the Philadelphia Redevelopment Authority and the Philadelphia Historical Commission in preservation planning for Society Hill and Washington Square West has not been matched by careful preservation planning in other areas of Philadelphia. In the 1970s, although colonial and early nineteenth-century buildings have usually been preserved, demolitions have often been the rule for Victorian structures. For example, the Market Street East commercial redevelopment has led to the destruction of many buildings in this old business district. Plans for Market Street East include a new underground railway tunnel and a new highway corridor, both of which will necessitate further demolitions. The underground train center will make unnecessary the Reading Terminal trainshed, the last surviving single-span trainshed in this country, and as a result it will probably be torn down. The new highway will isolate and disrupt the Chinatown neighborhood adjacent to Market Street East.

The destruction in Market Street East, as well as the earlier destruction of other nineteenth-century commercial buildings by the federal government to create the mall showcasing Independence Hall, reflects the city's lack of commitment to Victorian buildings. Demolitions carried out for expansion and other reasons by the University of Pennsylvania in West Philadelphia have also revealed a great insensitivity to these buildings. In general, late nineteenth-century buildings have suffered not only because of redevelopment, but also from functional superfluity. This has particularly become a problem for landmark church buildings that can no longer be maintained by the declining congregations; and it has affected nineteenth-century rowhouses that are of marginal use and are thus often allowed to deteriorate to an uninhabitable state. Both churches and rowhouses are frequently replaced by parking lots or vacant lots.

Because of its position in city government and the political pressures brought to bear on it, the historical commission has been unable to do much about this ongoing crisis for nineteenth-century buildings. The commission has given landmark designations to Victorian houses in the Spring Garden neighborhood, but the initiative for the preservation of these houses and for their

FIGURE 3.6 Spring Garden Victorians

designation has come from private individuals and from the Spring Garden Civic Association. The commission has also supported private efforts of the Old City Civic Association to save cast-iron buildings in the old commercial district to the east of Independence Mall. In the absence of a well-developed private preservation organization, the burden of protesting the destruction of nineteenth-century buildings has fallen on the local chapters of the Society of Architectural Historians and the American Institute of Architects, and on the Victorian Society. The Philadelphia architectural historians have been especially active in publicizing the crisis through a bimonthly newsletter and a weekly "Preservation Now" radio program on a local FM station. They have also sponsored tours and other educational activities to create support for the preservation of Victorian buildings.

The fixation on preserving colonial and early nineteenth-century buildings and the neglect of Victorian architecture are problems in other cities on the Eastern seaboard. In the Western states, by contrast, Victorian architecture is appreciated and preserved as the oldest building style in the cities. The recent interest in the buildings designed by Frank Furness and the costly restoration of Furness' 100-year-old Pennsylvania Academy of the Fine Arts may foreshadow a new appreciation of Victorian buildings and architects in Philadelphia. If this in turn leads to the preservation and restoration of more Victorian buildings, then the educational efforts of Philadelphia architectural historians, architects, and preservationists will have been successful.

The restoration of Society Hill marks a transition from the earliest experience with historic districts, as seen in Charleston and New Orleans, to the contemporary application of preservation techniques. The first historic districts developed the use of zoning and historic commissions; the later districts added the use of urban renewal and city planning practices. In contemporary historic districts any or all of these practices may be utilized.

Contemporary Practices in Charleston and New Orleans

As we are familiar with the early development of historic districts in Charleston and New Orleans, it is interesting to see how contemporary practices have affected the operation of these districts.

Both Charleston and New Orleans have recently had city planning studies done of their historic areas. These plans review the existing practice in the historic areas, place the areas in the context of the larger city, and make certain specific recommendations. They reveal not only recent historic district practices, but also the current status of the districts.

The Historic Preservation Plan for Charleston, completed in June 1974, was the outcome of three years of research by City Planning and Architectural Associates, Russell Wright, Carl Feiss, and the National Heritage Corporation.[7] The plan dealt with the entire peninsular area south of the Crosstown Expressway (U.S. Highway 17), including areas not presently included in the historic district. After reviewing the findings of previous surveys, the research group undertook a comprehensive historic architecture inventory of the area. The survey included driving every street, resurveying important sections on foot, mapping and photographing, documentation, and a partial survey of interiors. The survey results were analyzed and the buildings were rated exceptional, excellent, significant, or contributory. Also noted were buildings requiring further research, those adversely altered and requiring restoration, and those insignificant and thus suitable for redevelopment.

The research group used this inventory to supplement and refine, from a preservation point of view, the preliminary peninsular land use plan of 1973. On the basis of the inventory, the land use considerations, and the desirability of retaining the unique historic architecture and milieu, a series of recommendations were made and detailed in the preservation plan:

1. Official recognition and adoption of the historic architecture inventory to be administered by the Board of Architectural Review
2. Adoption of height limits in the study area
3. Adoption of a composite preservation index classifying buildings from excellent and significant to little architectural significance, based on the inventory
4. Adoption of a land use plan based on the preservation index to guide municipal actions and development in the historic area
5. Support of the passage of strong preservation legislation at the state level to strengthen preservation at the municipal level

and to authorize a local agency replacing the Board of Architectural Review to administer proposals made in the plan

6. Establishment of various additional preservation techniques (i.e., facade easements program, a revolving fund, and tax incentives) to be administered by the agency
7. Supplementary recommendations including (a) antilittering and weed control ordinance, (b) antibillboard ordinance, (c) code enforcement, (d) antineglect ordinance, (e) downtown revitalization program, and (f) design studies for neighborhoods, waterfront sections, and commercial sections.

Several concerns underlie these recommendations. First, the preservationists in Charleston would like to expand the area under historic control up to the crosstown expressway and adopt the inventory's description of historic resources in the area, thus providing a basis for decisions on alterations, demolitions, and development. Second, they would like to strengthen the legal framework by superseding the present zoning administration and the Board of Architectural Review with a preservation agency that has stronger legal powers supported by state legislation. Third, they would like to improve the economic position of preservation by shifting some of the burden from private groups, like the Historic Charleston Foundation or the Save Charleston Foundation, to a revolving fund easements program and a tax program partly funded by bonds or other public revenue and administered by the proposed agency. Fourth, they would like the cooperation of the city in this comprehensive preservation program through land use planning, height limits, code enforcement, antilitter, antineglect, and antibillboard ordinances in this comprehensive preservation program.

How are we to evaluate these recommendations and the concerns that underlie them? Preservation in Charleston has been successful for many reasons that go beyond the legal framework provided by the zoning and the Board of Architectural Review—the unique architecture, the unified social concern, the small size of the city. To this list we should also add the success of the Historic Charleston Foundation in organizing the rehabilitation of Ansonborough, supporting historic neighborhood organizations in Wraggsborough and in Harleston, and having these areas incorporated in the historic

FIGURE 3.7 (*above*) Historic Charleston Foundation headquarters, Nathaniel Russell House Museum; (*below*) Ansonborough houses being sold by the Historic Charleston Foundation for restoration

zone. Clearly, the private sector has contributed a great deal to making the zoning and architectural review process effective.

Nevertheless, the recommendations embody a shift in responsibility from the private to the public sector in areas of legal controls, economic resources, and further preservation planning. This shift is necessary because the private organizations have overextended themselves attempting to control the situation in threatened portions of the historic area. Of critical importance is the increasing pressure for development in the peninsular area that is driving up the price of real estate to a point where preservation may become too expensive for the private organizations to handle alone. The need for legal and planning controls also reflects this pressure, as a very few modern developments on a large scale could easily upset the entire balance of the historic area.

We must assume that the development threat is serious. Also, the preservationists of Charleston played a major role in the formulation of the preservation plan, and we can therefore expect that it embodies their viewpoint. As noted above, the very success of preservation encourages speculation and new development. Speculation makes preservation more difficult, and development, although it can be beneficial, can also engulf an historic area. The preservationists of Charleston have been careful to minimize speculation, and the preservation plan suggests that they are now turning their attention to the problem of development. In this effort to control development and land use in a way compatible with preservation, we can see that the scope of preservation itself is being broadened. Where preservation started with the historic house and then proceeded to the historic district, its advocates now propose a union of preservation goals and land use planning to encompass a good portion of the entire city.

The plan deals with other problems affecting the survival of Charleston buildings, namely, demolition through neglect and the lack of tax incentives for rehabilitation of historic structures. The plan proposes that neglect be cited by the city and, if repairs are not made, that they be carried out at city expense, with the cost placed as a lien on the property. For tax incentives for rehabilitation, the plan proposes a decrease in the tax rate to offset the cost of repairs. As it stands now improvements to a building increase the tax rate, thus acting to discourage the improvement of old properties. The problems of neglect and taxes have been noted by preservationists throughout the country; the remedies suggested in Charleston are like those proposed elsewhere.

As yet, the recommendations of the plan have not resulted in the creation of a preservation agency. However, the plan and the historic inventory are available to the public and will no doubt have an influence on the course of preservation in Charleston. The exact details of the plan may not be implemented, and the major impetus for preservation may remain with the private organizations. In fact, this may be for the best, for although the plan indicates that the scope of preservation discussion has broadened, the initiative and innovation that originate with the private organizations are still the mainstays of successful preservation.

Planning for the Vieux Carré

The *Plan and Program for the Preservation of the Vieux Carré,* carried out by the Bureau of Governmental Research for New Orleans and completed at the end of 1968, was funded through an Urban Renewal Demonstration Grant from the Department of Housing and Urban Development. The Vieux Carré report is more formidable than the Charleston plan. It consists of a summary and a seven-volume technical supplement covering the following topics: environmental survey; legal and administrative report; economic and social study; the Vieux Carré of New Orleans—its plan, its growth, its architecture; New Orleans central business district traffic study; evaluation of the effects of the proposed riverfront expressway; and technical report on the effects of the proposed riverfront expressway.[8]

The topics dealt with show that the study gave detailed consideration to the economic and social aspects of the Vieux Carré, the traffic in the quarter and adjacent areas, and the impact of a proposed expressway. The Charleston plan also dealt with economic and traffic questions, but on a much more limited scale.

It is impossible to review the report in its entirety here. Instead we shall examine the various technical concerns and recommendations as responses to the overall situation. Notwithstanding the historic and artistic character of the Vieux Carré, the quarter's problems have much the same sources as do Charleston's. There are two levels of √ problems: the technical difficulties that confront the Vieux Carré Commission in its administration of the historic district, and those that arise from the relationship of the historic district to the forces operating in the city as a whole.

The problems of the Vieux Carré Commission result from ineffective enforcement of its architectural controls and decisions, from demolition due to neglect in certain sections of the historic area, and from pressures for development that are hard to control. The study suggests the underlying difficulty in all of these areas is the weak legal footing of the commission and its lack of sufficient funding to carry out its work. As in the Charleston plan, a new preservation law and agency are proposed, with more power and better funding. To date, however, this has not transpired.

Without the solution proposed in the report, it is interesting to see how the Vieux Carré Commission "muddles through." In the area of architectural design and control, the commission is presented with a continuous stream of minor and major porposals; dealing with these takes the major portion of the commission's time and effort. The architectural committee, the most active of the commission's committees, must approve and inspect work in the quarter. Although this can go smoothly, it can also go badly when the committee and an owner do not agree on what should be done. An example may help to illustrate. A three-story building with a central courtyard is to be converted into a series of apartments. The owner does not live in the building and is mainly concerned with dividing the building into the maximum number of apartments while minimizing the cost of renovation. The commission can only control work done to the exterior and to the courtyard (an exterior surface). In the first go-round the owner seeks to close off a portion of the courtyard, claiming that there had been servants quarters there in the past. The committee finds no evidence of this and rejects enclosure. The owner proceeds without permit to alter a portion of the open stairwell onto the courtyard. During an inspection of other work a committee member notes this. At a later meeting, when the owner denies that any alteration has been made, the committee threatens to halt all further work until the alteration has been returned to its original appearance. The owner seems to agree, but at the next inspection, the committee finds that the alteration has not been undone. It also examines the wrought-iron balconies on the front of the building. The owner and his architect try to suggest that the wrought iron is not very old and that they should be allowed to replace it with a modern equivalent. The committee finds the ironwork quite old enough and favors restoration, but the owner demurs. At the meeting following the inspection, the matter of the alteration is again raised, the committee threatens, the owner demurs. And so on. The process is laborious and time-consuming; distrust and suspicion exacerbate the situation.

In general, the commission must depend upon goodwill and sympathy to achieve its goals. The historic area is too large to be continuously inspected. A sign that does not comply with the sign controls may go unnoticed for some time; when it is noticed the commission requests its removal, but more time may go by before the commission inspector checks to see if it has been removed. Entertainment advertisements on Bourbon Street illustrate this rather well. Three violation notices are sent before the commission goes to court about the problem. Of course, the commission can stop work on a noncomplying project, or it can force the removal of the sign; but these measures are ones of last resort, for their too frequent use would increase opposition to the controls.

In the last four years, the staff of the Vieux Carré Commission has doubled from six to thirteen positions, and its annual budget has tripled from $50,000 to $150,000. This has increased the capability of the commission to inspect for violations and the number cited has increased. However, the commission usually seeks to persuade property owners to comply, rather than to rush into court actions.

Demolition through neglect has been a considerable problem to the commission, as this is a tactic used by property owners seeking to demolish a building and replace it with some new development. Until 1972 the only options open to the commission in these cases were to allow demolition and new development, or to oppose demolition and seek court action against the property owner while further deterioration occurred. In 1972 the city established a $300,000 revolving fund for public restoration that would enable the commission to purchase, restore, and then sell structures threatened with demolition by neglect. This fund has provided a partial solution to the neglect impasse, for as a last resort, the commission can buy a

FIGURE 3.8   Vieux Carré Commission Office, Upper Pontalba Building

threatened structure. However, the resources of the fund are limited and cannot be relied on for more than a few critical cases:

> Government cannot and should not bear the full financial responsibility for the rehabilitation of the structures in the Vieux Carré—the long term vitality of the area is dependent on the existence of committed individuals who own and restore their buildings. However, there are circumstances where the dependence on the private market and the regulatory tools of government are not sufficient to assure the structural maintenance of certain properties. At those times it is incumbent upon the government to provide the last resort, to hold the line against demolition, to preserve the buildings of importance to the Vieux Carré and the community.[9]

Fortunately, the property values and private investment in the Vieux Carré have been increasing rapidly as demand for residences and apartments in the quarter increases, and as a result property owners have an incentive to rehabilitate and maintain their buildings.

While increasing property values and private investment may

work against demolition through neglect, at the same time they reflect the pressures for development that are at work in the Vieux Carré. These development pressures in turn reflect the increasing residential, commercial, and tourist demands made on the historic area. The residential pressures, resulting from the desirability of living in the quarter, can promote restoration, but can also lead to extensive subdivision of buildings into small apartments. This then places a heavy use burden on the building and may lead to deterioration. Residential demand may also lead to the conversion of deteriorated commercial buildings into apartments. This may be beneficial, but the displacement of light industry alters the character of activity in the quarter. A change is also seen in the increasing number of tourist and specialty shops. The tourist enchantment with the Vieux Carré has required the construction of a number of new hotels and motels in the district. These are designed in a style compatible with the existing architecture, but some of the older buildings have been replaced in the process:

> New construction is already creating serious disruptions to the historic district. Though a number of new structures have been built on vacant lots, others have replaced older buildings of architectural-historic importance. The vacant lots are being quickly used up, an indication that development pressure on existing structures will increase sharply in the near future. Commercial building to accommodate the Vieux Carré's growing tourist attraction thus threatens to erode the very authenticity of the Quarter that constitutes its essential tourist appeal.[10]

The Vieux Carré study predicts further development of the area as a specialty shopping and entertainment center for the city. These economic changes in the life of the quarter are bound to affect the *tout ensemble*.

Development pressures in the historic district cannot be isolated from development in the city as a whole. The evolution of the Vieux Carré into a tourist-oriented, specialty-shop, and fashionable residence area should be seen as part of the specialization and separation of functions occurring citywide. This sorting out of industry, residence, and commerce centers has been encouraged in city planning and zoning; it is hardly unique to New Orleans. Within this scheme, historic areas seem inevitably to evolve into the kind of specialized district that is developing in the Vieux Carré.

This specialization and separation of functions are based on quick transportation, frequently on an automobile freeway system. Historic areas can pose a problem to these systems because of their narrow streets, or because they are in the way of a freeway route. The Vieux Carré has posed both of these problems to the larger city; or to look at it the other way around, street traffic congestion and proposed highway construction are both threats to the historic district.

The preservation plan was in part undertaken to study and minimize the impact of a proposed riverfront expressway on the Vieux Carré. The proposals in the plan for relief of traffic congestion in the quarter were predicated on the construction of this expressway, which was expected to divert traffic then traveling through the area. With the decreased traffic the plan recommended the closing of some of the narrow internal streets, forcing the traffic onto larger streets circulating around the quarter.

Many preservationists viewed the proposed riverfront expressway, which would have run between the Vieux Carré and the river, as a disruption of the historic setting. Judging from the outcome of similar riverfront freeways in other cities, the expressway would have cut the Vieux Carré off from the river. However, the preservation plan did propose that the freeway be placed underground for the section next to the Vieux Carré and that residential development and parks be planned for the surrounding riverfront area. Despite these ameliorative plans, the President's Advisory Council on Historic Preservation found that the expressway would have a negative impact on the Vieux Carré, and consequently the secretary of the Department of Transportation halted the planning for it in 1968.

The elimination of the expressway was certainly important for the future of the Vieux Carré, but the traffic problem remains unresolved. In following some of the suggestions of the preservation plan, the commission has stopped auto traffic on three sides of Jackson Square and a block of Exchange Alley, and restricted it during certain hours on Bourbon and Royal streets, thus creating pedestrian malls on these streets. Large buses have been routed out of the interior of the quarter to Decatur and Rampart streets at the periphery, and a minibus service has been initiated in their place. New parking facilities have also been created. Nevertheless, traffic in the quarter remains heavy.

Leaving aside these particular problems of the Vieux Carré Commission and the historic district, the preservation plan embodied several proposals for major improvements in the historic area, and several of these have been carried out since 1968. One might not think that improvements to an historic area in keeping with its historic character would cause problems, but the improvements undertaken in the Vieux Carré have been controversial. Many of the improvements have centered on the Jackson Square area, particularly the mall around the square, including the renovation of the city-owned Upper Pontalba Building facing on the square, the rehabilitation of the city-operated French Market complex adjacent to the square, and the development of the Washington Artillery Park overlooking the river. These renovations have faced two major criticisms. First, long-term tenants in the Pontalba and the French Market, such as the local Colonial Dames organization, the Spring Fiesta Committee, and the nearly historic Morning Call coffee stand, were forced out of their quarters by the high-rent schedules planned for the renovated buildings. The effect of this on the market in particular angered many people:

> In a way, this exodus has had a greater effect on the appearance of the market than the physical change. Some of the old tenants with roots in the community ran very informal operations, so that a relaxed, if not lethargic, atmosphere pervaded the area.
>
> Since the clean-up campaign of the '30's, the market had slowly decayed again to the stage of unkempt charm which many attributed to the tender ravages of great age. It had attained again that "left bank" quality which is apparently a necessary ingredient for romance.... At some imperceptible point, the deteriorated quality had become an integral part of people's perception of the market as an institution. Thus, the removal of the easy-going quality and the clearing up of the mess seems to have traumatized some people to the point of launching a serious and desperate campaign to save the last remaining messy element, the tattered awning over the Cafe du Monde.[11]

The second criticism of the renovations is a response to the clean and new appearance that characterizes the mall, the Pontalba, the

FIGURE 3.9 (*above* and *below*) The French Market

slickness

market, and the Artillery Park. "It is upsetting that restoration always seems to kill the spirit that a building possesses as a semi-ruin. It makes the building slick and pretentious. It homogenizes the building, smoothing over the roughness, hardening the softness, and removing all the subtlety of the textural and color variations. In short, a restored building no longer looks old; it looks new."[12] In the New Orleans climate, these "new" buildings should quickly weather into place, but the new quality of restoration work is not isolated to New Orleans. It recalls the "vandalism of finishing" to which the British preservationists objected in the nineteenth century and seems to be a continuing tendency in the restoration process. In American work, new and slick renovation is associated with commercial rehabilitation and is noticeable in the improvements around Jackson Square. The final appearance of the square reflects this style of renovation as well as the professional effort to follow the evidence of architectural history in the restorations.

The operations and problems of the Vieux Carré Commission give an idea of what to expect in a contemporary historic district. Other developments in New Orleans indicate the extension of preservation activity beyond the Vieux Carré. In Charleston, the historic district has been expanded through the work of the Historic Charleston Foundation and neighborhood organizations to include areas adjoining the original historic district. In New Orleans, the boundaries of the Vieux Carré Historic District are set down in the state constitution, and these have not been expanded. Nevertheless, preservationists have branched out into adjoining historic areas, and the city government has established a municipal Historic Districts Commission both to regulate new historic districts beyond the Vieux Carré and to conduct studies leading to their establishment. Two new districts have already been designated, the Saint Charles Avenue and the Lower Garden districts. In addition, the historic areas of the central business core are being considered for designation as an office buildings district, a warehouse district, and a Lafayette Square District.

This expansion of historic districts has come about in several ways that suggest the active work of New Orleans preservationists. In 1965 the Friends of the Cabildo wrote a series of books on New Orleans architecture; the first four were on the Lower Garden District, the American sector (central business district), the cemeteries, and the

Creole faubourgs. The books provide architectural histories of the areas, examples of typical forms of buildings well illustrated with photographs and drawings, and an architectural inventory. In addition to these books the Friends of the Cabildo and the Junior League have sponsored Building Watchers Tours to the various areas to further acquaint the public with the historic architecture. The Junior League has also sponsored and funded a Preservation Resource Center to serve as a clearinghouse for information, to organize workshops and exhibitions, and to carry out related programs. The expressed intention of these activities is to stimulate public appreciation of the historic areas so that they will not be lost out of ignorance of their existence.

If the new districts can be taken as evidence, the work of the Friends of the Cabildo and the Junior League have found a sympathetic echo in the neighborhood organizations of those areas. An outstanding example of neighborhood effort for preservation can be seen in the activities of the Coliseum Square Association in the Lower Garden District. Coliseum Square, the park, and the residences surrounding it exemplify antebellum New Orleans. There was little building after the war, and until the demolitions of the past decade the area remained unchanged if increasingly deteriorated. The book on the Lower Garden District appeared in 1971, and several houses on Coliseum Square were purchased and restored by individuals associated with the Friends of the Cabildo or the Louisiana Landmarks Society. The Coliseum Square Association was formed, and by publicizing the restorations, its members encouraged others in the neighborhood to paint and repair their houses. Several overly subdivided residences were purchased by one enthusiast, refurbished into duplex apartments, and rented. The association started a house tour and also compiled an inventory of the area that was submitted to the Historic District Commission when the area was proposed as an historic district. The association has also lobbied with the city government to have the Coliseum Square park renovated. The effectiveness of the association has been enhanced by the help of the young professionals, architects and lawyers, who have been attracted to the area, and by the support of groups from outside the area.

In many ways preservation in the Lower Garden District is an interesting social experiment as well as a preservation effort. While

FIGURE 3.10   Coliseum Square, Lower Garden District

the Saint Charles Avenue area, and in large measure the Vieux Carré, are exclusive and expensive neighborhoods, the Lower Garden District is predominantly a poor area. Thus the success of the preservation effort depends not only on the renovation of the buildings, but also on the goodwill of the neighborhood's black residents. With the help of new professional residents, the Coliseum Square Association has developed the kind of planning and leadership that are needed to upgrade a neighborhood and make it an attractive place to live. The association has helped to define and strengthen the image of the neighborhood as seen by the larger city, and the residents themselves have gained confidence through this new perception of their area. In the public's mind renovation, public order, and desirability of an area are equated, as are deterioration, crime, and abandonment. These are subjective factors, but they are at play in the effort for restoration. The momentum achieved in Coliseum Square could cease if the poorer residents of the area become hostile to the preservationists or if the preservation effort is too successful, drawing in speculators and changing the area into another exclusive enclave. Only a moderate success, upgrading the neighborhood but keeping its present mixed composition, can create the kind of neighborhood renovation that preservationists throughout the country have been working toward. For this reason, the progress of the Lower Garden District should be closely watched.

The Vieux Carré and other historic districts in New Orleans demonstrate that preservation has become a complex social activity involving a variety of public commissions and private organizations. The districts illustrate one set of responses to preservation goals, often involving public commissions in the administration, planning, and problems of the districts, and the private organizations in defining, supporting, and extending them. In the absence of an already existing historic district, private organizations in other cities are developing other sets of responses to preservation goals.

4. INNOVATIVE APPROACHES:
Financing and Promotion of Preservation

In the last decade private organizations and individual preservationists have developed several innovative approaches to secure the future of old buildings. These approaches are independent of the establishment of historic districts, but they often lead to such an outcome. The successful Historic Savannah Foundation can illustrate several of these innovations.

Historic Savannah Foundation

Savannah, Georgia, is a small city of 118,000 inhabitants; it is also an old and historic city first settled in 1733. The plan of the city laid down by General James Oglethorpe, founder of the colony, provided for the setting aside of a public square as each ward was developed. This plan was followed for a century resulting in twenty-two squares, and a unique planning and architectural heritage for the city. As Savannah was not so prominent a city as Charleston, the buildings around the squares are not so grand; nevertheless, they are excellent material for the architectural historian and the preservationist.

As Savannah grew in the nineteenth and twentieth centuries, the oldest part of the city passed gradually into decay. A few of the squares were cut through for streets; others simply went to seed. Some of the houses were demolished also for their Savannah gray bricks, much favored by builders for houses in the newer areas of the city. Fortunately, due to the slow growth of Savannah, these inroads were minor until after World War II, when, in pace with the nationwide boom, pressures for new development, parking lots, and Savannah gray bricks began to take an increasing toll in the historic zone.

Preservation in Savannah began slowly after World War II when Mary Hillyer, wife of the Savannah Gas Company president, became interested in some dilapitated buildings on property belonging to the company. These buildings, known as the Trustee's Garden Village, were gradually restored through the Hillyers' efforts, and when completed in 1961, more than thirty buildings had been saved and given new residential or commercial uses. An annual tour of homes, initiated in 1939 by the women of Christ Episcopal Church, has gradually contributed also to the growth of preservation sentiments in the city. Today the annual event has become a formidable affair with three different tours and a large and detailed tour information insert in the *Savannah Morning News–Evening Press*. Another forerunner of preservation was the purchase of the Juliette Gordon Low House in 1953 by the Girl Scouts of America, for use as a Southern regional headquarters and historic house (Fig. 2.1, p. 33). The house was restored in 1956 and since then has been visited by many Girl Scout troops and by the general public. The house is also used for a museum aides seminar for senior scouts. The GSA subsequently purchased an adjoining old building for office use; both houses and the garden have been further restored through the work of the organization and gifts from Girl Scouts throughout the country. Both the Trustee's Garden Village and the Low house were isolated efforts that did not involve the general public; but both did break ground for later work.

The Historic Savannah Foundation, formed in 1954, was the outgrowth of a series of preservation crises in the city. In 1951 the city proposed a street be put through the squares on Habersham Street; however, a Society for the Preservation of the Squares of Savannah was formed and successfully opposed the bisection. In 1954 the historic Old City Market, built on the site of one of the original squares, was demolished and replaced by a multitier parking structure. This was opposed unsuccessfully by many Savannahans, and a ball organized by Mrs. Anna Hunter was held in the market prior to its demolition. The last straw came when a funeral home proposed to tear down the Davenport House on Columbia Square for a parking lot. Mrs. Hunter and several other women organized the Historic Savannah Foundation and bought the house. Deeded to a nonpreservation organization, it was later turned over to the foundation, which has restored the house and uses the ground floor as a headquarters. In its first years, the organization reacted to

FIGURE 4.1   Historic Savannah Foundation headquarters, Isaiah Davenport House Museum

preservation crises as they arose. As late as 1959 the property values remained depressed in the historic areas and young couples with children were reluctant to move into the old center of the city.

Up to this point, preservation in Savannah had not departed from traditional approaches, but this changed rapidly after 1959 when several experienced leaders in the business community became involved with the foundation. In the fall of 1959 the foundation had tried unsuccessfully to save Marshall Row, an abandoned row of houses. Demolition seemed certain, but

> At the last minute, after the wrecker had already demolished the carriage houses that stood behind the old magnificent houses, Leopold Adler II, a young investment banker, bargained with the owner of the property and bought the land on which the houses stood for $45,000. Then he went to the demolition company that had bought the houses for the brick. . . . The wrecker had paid $6,000 for the valuable brick, but Mr. Adler bought the "standing" bricks for $9,000. Since the

owner of the property did not want to sell his land to Historic Savannah, Mr. Adler found three other businessmen to sign a deed along with him and purchased the land.[1]

Following this cliff-hanger a steering committee of business men and women active in the Historic Savannah Foundation was organized to formulate an action program for the organization. The program branched out in three directions: a tourist development program, an inventory of the historic area, and a revolving redevelopment fund for active intervention in the historic area. Together, these three proved to be a successful combination.

The tourist development program was intended to win over the Savannah business community by convincing them of the economic benefits of expanded tourism. A tourist and convention bureau was established in the Savannah Chamber of Commerce; and the chamber with the Historic Savannah Foundation sponsored a report by Thomas G. McCaskey, a vice-president of Colonial Williamsburg and an authority on travel. The McCaskey Report was issued in 1965 and was widely circulated. It provided an assessment of Savannah's potential for tourism that supported the ideas the tourist bureau had been developing, and together they provided an image of the future of Savannah that appealed to many in the business community.

Tourism is often suggested today as one of the benefits that can accrue from preservation; however, this may create false hopes in a community that has few possibilities for developing tourism, and may in the long run have adverse consequences for preservation if the promised tourists do not materialize. Not every city can be a tourist destination. An examination of Savannah's suitability to this role will illustrate how to assess the potential value of tourism to other towns.

The McCaskey Report detailed the steps for the tourist development program in Savannah and explained how to realize it. The potential of the city for tourism rests on its unique historic, commercial, and architectural past; but this must be clearly articulated in a series of city images to be presented to the touring public in regional advertisements, articles in travel magazines and newspaper travel sections, a short film, and other public relations formats. McCaskey suggested the following image themes for Savannah: "Colonial Capital of Georgia; Throne of King Cotton; City of Famous Historic Park Greens and Squares."[2] Once the city

FIGURE 4.2 Savannah Visitors' Center and Chamber of Commerce—restored railroad station

image is established through this public relations campaign, then the city must follow through by first alerting (via highway signs and billboards) the auto traveler that he is near unique and historic Savannah, and then, by providing the visitor with the kind of experiences he has been led to expect. This last, but very important aspect, includes the development of sufficient historic houses, displays, and museums open to the public; the arrangement of a clearly marked tour route, brochures, and a visitor's center for tourist orientation; encouragement of restaurants that carry through the historic theme; and finally provision of pleasant accommodations, parking facilities, and other amenities for the visitor. The McCaskey Report emphasized the pragmatics of developing the tourist program; this emphasis indicates some of the elements that create a potential for tourism.

To begin with, a town must be able to project a clear and distinctive image to the touring public. This image is not a random concoction. Most cities and towns have some kind of image, whether industrial, scenic, architectural, or historic. The question for preservationists is whether a town's historic and architectural image can be sufficiently developed to hold the tourist's interest. This depends on two factors—the historic and architectural resources of the town and competing images of the town. If the historic and architectural resources are sparse, a town may well seek to preserve them. However, they would probably not sustain a tourist's interest for more than an hour or two, even with the tourist development program. Of course, in this case the preserved buildings might be tied in with some other town image, such as scenery, beaches, or climate, to heighten the attraction for tourists; but then preservation is only an ancillary element for the town's image. On the other hand, some image factors, such as industry or nightlife, may compete with preservation to such an extent that, although historic and architectural resources are extensive and preservationists are active in saving city neighborhoods and commercial buildings, preservation is still not part of the tourist image of the city. One thinks of historic Boston, for example, but not of historic Pittsburgh. Both cities have active preservation movements, yet for Pittsburgh the industrial image of steel and glass manufacture, the sports image of Three River Stadium and the Pittsburgh Steelers, and the cultural image of Carnegie Library and the University of Pittsburgh's Tower of Learning preclude other images. In Pittsburgh, the tourist expects to see industrial plants, not row houses. For this reason, the Pittsburgh Historic Landmarks Foundation appeals primarily to residents and has not proposed tourism as a major benefit of preservation.

If it is judged that the city image will allow or support preservation as a major tourist appeal, then the way is clear for a campaign to publicize the image and for planned development of the town's historic resources to meet the tourist's expectations. In publicizing an historic image and planning development to support it, a town must be prepared for the consequences of preservation dependent on tourists—the frequent presence of groups of strangers wandering in and about the areas marked on the historic tour and the opening to visitation of houses in the historic area. These strangers must be put at ease by friendly hosts and guides and must feel safe so that they can enter into the spirit of the historic environment they have come to see. An historic area that is still deteriorated and slumlike is not ready for most tourists. Thus a community must be prepared to make an initial investment in sidewalk, park, and building rehabilitation before the tourists can be invited in. Tourists are interested in some work in progress, and this can be included in an historic tour; but completely undeveloped historic areas hold little for them.

In Savannah the tourist development program could be carried out with relative ease. Savannah had been a popular tourist destination in the 1930s with tourist attractions in and around the city—Telfair Academy, Christ Church, Colonial Dawes House, Fort Pulaski, Tyber Beach, and Fort McAllister. The McCaskey Report focused attention on the historic zone of the city and suggested how, with the sharpening of the tourist image and with the development of more attractions and an area tour, tourism would flourish. The recommendations depended upon the restoration of the historic area and thus aided the Historic Savannah Foundation in its efforts for preservation.

As the second step in its program, the Historic Savannah Foundation completed in 1962 a survey and inventory of historic buildings in the two-and-one-half-square-mile center of the city. The foundation used the survey to inform preservationists and the business community of significant buildings, and their numbers supported arguments for the tourist potential of the area. The inventory was published in 1968 in a volume entitled *Historic Savannah,* and in 1973 was the basis for historic district zoning of the area. An inventory, a straightforward tool for alerting the public to existing historic resources, served this purpose well in Savannah.

With the inventory, the Historic Savannah Foundation identified areas of the historic core requiring special attention. To ensure their preservation the foundation embarked on the third part of its program, a revolving redevelopment fund for the purchase of properties. This was combined with an active resale program, modeled on new housing development promotions, that ensured the rehabilitation of the building by the new owner and freed the revolving fund monies for further use.

The revolving fund was modeled on a similar program already developed in Charleston, where a $100,000 fund-raising drive had been undertaken in 1957. The fund was to be used for a demonstration area project outside of Charleston's historic district. In 1959, with the fund-raising completed, the Historic Charleston Foundation chose

FIGURE 4.3   Pulaski Square

Ansonborough as the target area. At the time Ansonborough was a slum with a high concentration of antebellum buildings. Using the fund, the foundation purchased and resold them to private parties with an attached covenant requiring exterior restoration and maintenance. The foundation purchased and resold over fifty buildings, often at a small loss. Publicity led others in the area to improve their property as well, or to sell to those who would. In 1966 the boundary of the historic district was expanded to include Ansonborough; by that time both property values and the tax base had greatly increased. Since then the revolving fund has been replenished by donations, and the area project approach has been extended to Radcliffeborough and to Wraggsborough.

The Historic Savannah Foundation sought to emulate Charleston's success with a $200,000 fund of its own. The foundation chose as its target area Pulaski Square, a deteriorated neighborhood that had shown excellent historic resources in the inventory. Agents for the Historic Savannah Foundation bought fifty-four properties in the area in 1964 and 1965 and sold them with preservation covenants. A six-page explanatory brochure, weekend tours, and signs designating the area as the Pulaski Square–West Jones Street Redevelopment Project were used to publicize the effort. These promotional techniques were suggested by J. Reid Williamson, a successful suburban developer, who had become executive director of the Historic Savannah Foundation. Leopold Adler II, president of the organization, encouraged this approach as it ensured a quick turnover of properties and a maximum utilization of the revolving fund. The financial burden of actual restoration was transferred to the new private owner. The foundation thus sought only to purchase and quickly resell the building with the inclusion of a covenant insuring preservation.

In theory, the use of a revolving fund is not complicated. The $200,000 fund of the Historic Savannah Foundation deposited in Savannah banks sympathetic to preservation was used to establish a credit line of potentially much greater value. The amount of credit a bank will extend to an organization is discretionary. In some cases, where banks have been unsympathetic, they have required that all loans for preservation be secured with securities or personal property of equivalent value. At such times preservationists may have had to mortgage their own property in order to obtain a loan to save a building. In Savannah, however, once the revolving fund was established, this was not the case. As several business leaders and bank officers were managing the revolving fund for the foundation, they were able to explain their program to the local banks and establish lines of credit worth considerably more than $200,000.

Even with this expanded credit, however, the Historic Savannah Foundation would only have been able to buy five to ten buildings if they intended to keep them and pay out the mortgages. This would have had some impact on the historic area, but not as much as the course taken. With the aid of the friendly banks, the foundation could purchase properties, tying up a small amount of money to obtain the mortgage loan and paying only the loan interest for several months. The foundation sought to resell the property during those months, thus reestablishing its credit position less the interest costs and any loss on the property. Options and sales contracts were also used by the foundation to control and transfer properties at minimal cost. In this fashion the foundation was able to buy and sell fifty properties in Pulaski Square with its $200,000 revolving fund. In 1967, the Historic Savannah Foundation launched a $500,000 fund drive, with $350,000 to go into its revolving fund. They also published and distributed a brochure, *Half-a-Heritage,* to show what had been accomplished and what remained to be done. With the additional funds, the foundation was able to intervene at any point in the historic area where buildings might be threatened and to undertake another area project around Monterey Square.

The endeavors of the Historic Savannah Foundation in the historic core were not without support from other sectors of the community. Several private individuals bought and restored sets of houses. The city government committed itself to preservation by moving some administrative offices into the old Factors' Walk commercial buildings along the riverfront and by sponsoring the Troup Trust Urban Renewal Project in the historic area. Restoration and development in this renewal area was guided by a strict design analysis based on sixteen criteria:

1. Height
2. Proportion of buildings' front facades
3. Proportion of openings within the facade
4. Rhythm of solids to voids in front facade
5. Rhythm of spacing of buildings on streets
6. Rhythm of entrance and/or porch projections
7. Relationship of materials
8. Relationship of textures
9. Relationship of color
10. Relationship of architectural details
11. Relationship of roof shapes
12. Walls of continuity
13. Relationship of landscaping
14. Ground cover
15. Scale
16. Directional expression of front elevation[3]

These design criteria were intended to identify characteristic historic and architectural elements. They influenced city policy in the historic area after 1966 and were part of the historic district zoning adopted in 1973.

The chamber of commerce has also participated in preservation by restoring Savannah's old railroad station as both a visitor's center and chamber office. This location for the tourist center, with its ample parking space, had been recommended in the McCaskey Report and should in time encourage the restoration of other old buildings near the station.

The success of the restoration efforts in the historic core of Savannah has been seen in the raised property values and tax base, in the tremendous increase in tourism, and in the cessation of most demolition threats in the area. Several things remain to be done—the restoration of commercial buildings on Broughton Street like that sponsored by the Historic Savannah Foundation on West Congress

Street; the closing of portions of Montgomery Street that bisect two squares; and the further restoration of buildings in some of the historic area. However, the active use of the revolving fund as seen in the 1960s is no longer a foundation policy. The Historic Savannah Foundation has returned to a more traditional form of preservation by purchasing the William Scarborough House and financing its restoration.

Some of the foundation members, led by former president Adler, have remained interested in area-wide preservation and have turned their attention to the low-income Victorian district south of the historic core. Incorporated as the Savannah Landmark Rehabilitation Project, they have proposed the renovation of the Victorian buildings using community redevelopment block grants and loan funds. The emphasis of this proposal is on the upgrading of low-income housing without dislocating the low-income residents to other areas.

FIGURE 4.4 Savannah Victorians

As a deterioriated area, several alternatives can be envisioned for the Victorian neighborhood. If the area is allowed to deteriorate further, demolition of buildings and their replacement by apartment and commercial buildings will ensue, with some displacement of the present low-income population. If private owners or speculators begin restoration in the area, low-income residents will be displaced, and the area will undergo a gentrification process like that which has occurred in the historic district; that is, spiraling property values and tax rates will force low-income groups out of the area. A third possibility, suggested by the Savannah Landmark Rehabilitation Project, is a subsidized rehabilitation program that will result in restored buildings owned by their former tenants. If this third approach is not carried through, one of the others is likely.

The rehabilitation project, termed Project SNAP, proposes the following goals:

1. To keep the present residents in the neighborhood;
2. To bring housing units up to minimum standard code;
3. To design a program of conversion to tenant ownership;
4. To promote the use of minority contractors and neighborhood workers and craftsmen;
5. To involve tenants and neighborhood residents in the management process;
6. To seek the technical assistance of existing housing agencies in Savannah.[4]

There are several assumptions embedded in these goals. Low-income families, whether owners or tenants, are often too poor to maintain their housing. For the welfare of the entire city, as well as for the welfare of the low-income families, this lack of funds should be overcome through a subsidy program, using federal funds funneled through local agencies. The outcome of this subsidy program should not only be rehabilitation of housing units, but also conversion of tenants into owners as the best way of ensuring continued maintenance of the property. Finally, the rehabilitation program should be used to refine the skills of neighborhood workers and craftsmen to benefit neighborhood firms and to develop community organization and leadership through involvement in managing the program.

The Project SNAP proposal seeks to rehabilitate 600 housing units over a six-year period, a number comparable to that achieved in the historic area by the Historic Savannah Foundation revolving fund and private investment. The proposal indicates the thinking of some preservationists who have been concerned about the dislocation of low-income groups from historic districts and have been seeking an alternative route to preservation.

Pittsburgh History and Landmarks Foundation

In Savannah, and in Charleston, revolving funds have been used primarily to purchase buildings and to quickly resell them to private parties for restoration. Recently, preservationists have noted that gentrification, displacement of lower- by middle-income residents, has been a social consequence of this practice, and they have tried to devise ways to keep members of varying income groups in areas undergoing preservation. In this new concern, the pioneering work of Pittsburgh preservationists in inner-city neighborhoods has drawn considerable attention. Using techniques similar to those used in Savannah, the Pittsburgh History and Landmarks Foundation (PHLF) has tried to achieve both preservation goals and retention of a neighborhood's income mix. In using their revolving fund, the foundation has aimed not at quick resale and restoration, but instead at restoration that stabilizes the neighborhood and encourages residents to repair their own property. The property owned by PHLF may be held for some time, leased or rented at an artifically low rate, or it may be sold. The decision on what action to take is based on social as well as architectural considerations.

In comparison with Charleston and Savannah, where preservation has resulted in exclusive neighborhoods and attractions for the tourist, in Pittsburgh the outcome has been different. Charleston and Savannah are small, and both white and black residents have a longstanding heritage in their communities. Pittsburgh, on the other hand, is a large industrial city, and a majority of its citizens migrated to the city within the last 100 years—the whites coming mostly from Eastern Europe, the blacks from the rural South. Although both groups have worked in the city's steel industry, which would not have developed without them, their relation to other aspects of the city's heritage is attenuated.

In Charleston and Savannah, as well as in New Orleans and Santa Fe, one thinks naturally and foremost of mood, color, ambience, history, and thus of preservation. This is not true in Pittsburgh, and any examination of the history of the city presents a different picture. First, Pittsburgh is industry, and not just any industry—but steel. The company names are the legend and heritage of Pittsburgh: Carnegie, Jones and Laughlin, Crucible, and U.S. Steel. And with the industry, which developed rapidly after the 1870s, came industrial slums and industrial pollution. By the turn of the century, living and working conditions in Pittsburgh had become almost intolerable. This was fully documented in one of the first comprehensive social surveys—the Pittsburgh Survey of 1907-08. Although charitable foundations established by the industrial elite made some ameliorative efforts—the Carnegie libraries, for example—working conditions did not improve until the 1930s when federal regulations and unionization set new health and safety standards. Housing and environmental conditions were not improved until after World War II.

During the years after 1945, a new generation of business leaders, led by Richard King Mellon, organized the Allegheny Conference for Community Development, which undertook to reverse the impending economic decline of Pittsburgh through a many-sided assault on the city's problems. Many of the proposed solutions had been planned and discussed in the 1920s and 1930s, but the Allegheny conference took rapid action. The conference programs included smoke control, flood control, development of an historic park at the confluence of the Monongahela and Allegheny rivers, redevelopment of the Golden Triangle central business district, highway construction, and housing renewal. Several of the programs required state support and involvement through ten bills presented to the state legislature in 1946, of which eight passed.[5] Municipal involvement in the programs came about through the establishment of an Urban Redevelopment Authority (URA). The results of this development effort, known as the Pittsburgh Renaissance, ensured the economic viability of the city and considerably improved the environment.

The activities of the redevelopment authority in both development and housing bear directly on the preservation effort in Pittsburgh. In the 1950s and 1960s, the URA, like similar redevelopment authorities in other cities, made extensive use of the practice of condemnation and complete clearance. This was often directed at black slum areas in the city; thus, the black community was the first to oppose it, favoring instead a program of housing rehabilitation. Preservationists in Pittsburgh, a small group at first, also opposed total clearance although for different reasons. The preservation program that evolved reflects this common interest in building rehabilitation.

While preservation had a high priority for part of the local elite in Charleston and Savannah, it received little notice in Pittsburgh until the organization of the Pittsburgh History and Landmarks Foundation late in 1964. Arthur Ziegler, Jr., one of the founders of the foundation and often its leader, has described its beginnings.

> On a late winter day in 1964 on Liverpool Street, in a black ghetto area James D. Van Trump and Arthur P. Ziegler, Jr., discouraged by the enormity of local architectural losses through urban redevelopment and general indifference, were walking along this sadly sagging late Victorian avenue. As rays from the falling sun picked out the detailing of the gingerbread porches, the two men, moved by the beauty amidst the squalor, resolved to find an alternative to redevelopment by demolition. PHLF . . . from the outset had a deep commitment to finding means to revitalize neighborhoods without removing either historic buildings or the inhabitants.[6]

Liverpool Street was to be the first preservation project of the foundation.

The preservation program developed by PHLF has been adaptive and pragmatic; it has made virtues of the necessities of the Pittsburgh situation, and it is in this that it has something to offer to preservationists in other large industrial cities. From the beginning, the main concern of PHLF, aside from some efforts for larger public commercial buildings, was to preserve domestic and commercial vernacular buildings of the late nineteenth century, buildings modest both historically and architecturally. In most cases these buildings were to be found in black, white, or mixed working-class neighborhoods. Pittsburgh residential segregation patterns did not for the most part encourage middle-class movement into working-class neighborhoods, white movement into black neighborhoods, or vice versa.[7] As a result, PHLF was not to have the problem of resident displacement, with the exception of the Mexican War Streets, a mixed neighborhood near the Allegheny Center Shopping Mall. The usual modesty of the historic architecture and the social patterns of residence in the city worked against the kind of preservation that occurred in Charleston or Savannah; however, PHLF was able to turn this fact to its advantage.

The program developed by PHLF emphasized community involvement and organization for preservation, the judicious use of a revolving fund for demonstration buildings, the use of public funds for low-interest loans and rent subsidies, and the stimulation of historic, architectural and community awareness through publications, exhibitions, and tours.

As stated above, the first area to receive PHLF attention was Liverpool Street, a black ghetto neighborhood in the Manchester district. The houses on the street were considered the best remaining examples of Victorian housing in the city. PHLF purchased two buildings on Liverpool Street and rehabilitated one of them; the other they held pending rehabilitation with funds from the federal leased housing program. PHLF worked with landlords, tenants, and the community organization to make minor improvements, such as painting foundations and window boxes, and street clearing. This self-help program moved slowly, while major work awaited some arrangement of public funding. The community opposed white movement into the area, and this eliminated the possibility of privately funded rehabilitation. Between 1964 and 1970, PHLF worked with the redevelopment authority to arrange for federal grants and loans under existing HUD programs; most details were set when a federal funding freeze stopped further action. During the freeze, several buildings in the Manchester area held by URA for rehabilitation deteriorated further and had to be demolished. A ten-house starter program has finally begun through the city neighborhood housing program, but the long delay in obtaining public funding has been costly in terms of architecture and in terms of community disappointment. Although Liverpool Street remains intact, the surrounding Manchester area presents the all too familiar picture of deteriorated buildings amidst vacant lots.

The problems that the PHLF had on Liverpool Street can be traced to the difficulty of obtaining public funds for rehabilitation. The other aspects of the PHLF program—demonstration projects with PHLF funds, community involvement and self-help, publication of a study of Liverpool Street as the second issue of the *Stones of Pittsburgh*—worked smoothly and stimulated neighborhood interest

FIGURE 4.5 (*above* and *below*) Liverpool Street

in preservation. But the absence of private investment and the shortage of public funds proved to be a considerable stumbling block.

While work on Liverpool Street moved slowly, the PHLF turned its attention to a second area, the Mexican War Streets, near the Allegheny Center Mall (itself a clearance and redevelopment project of the URA). The buildings on the Mexican War Streets were on a smaller scale than those on Liverpool Street, and the neighborhood had a mixed racial and income makeup:

> By 1966 it was a mixture of young and old, white and black, home owners and slum rooming house dwellers, poor to middle-income residents. Many buildings were badly blighted. The old-time residents were abandoning their houses to slumlords, and a final collapse seemed inevitable as things were going.
>
> After completing a study of the neighborhood, PHLF concluded that revitalization was possible without official urban redevelopment funds if:
> 1. The slumlords could be bought out.
> 2. Overcrowding in rooming houses could be eliminated and tenants relocated, as appropriate, to public housing or other units in the area.
> 3. Housing for low-income families could be improved.
> 4. New, particularly young, working residents could be attracted to move to the area.
> 5. The exodus of old-time home owners could be stopped.[8]

As the neighborhood appeared to be in transition, tending toward a rooming house slum, PHLF tried to reverse this process by choosing anchor buildings for rehabilitation. PHLF again began by purchasing and rehabilitating a house in the area, using money from the revolving fund established in 1966 with grants from local foundations. The first building bought and restored was an absentee-owned rooming house surrounded by privately owned residences. By reversing the downward course of the large rooming house and attracting new young tenants to the area, PHLF encouraged optimism in the owners of the surrounding residences. They, in turn, began to fix up and paint their houses giving a new stability to the block. PHLF used this tactic repeatedly in the Mexican War Streets, singling out anchor properties on each block for rehabilitation and depending on neighborhood residents to follow through on their buildings.

Buildings that the foundation had renovated were resold to private parties, leased to low-income residents under a leased housing program with the Pittsburgh Housing Authority, or let at low rents to neighborhood residents with any resulting loss charged against the revolving fund. In this way PHLF was able to sustain the low-income composition of the neighborhood while carrying out preservation.

As another part of its program, PHLF helped residents organize a neighborhood association to participate in the preservation process and to deal with area problems. PHLF has also sponsored annual tours and publicized the area's restoration in the newspapers and on television. These evidences of outside interest and involvement in the neighborhood are not to be underestimated as factors in creating community pride among the residents. By putting the Mexican War Streets on the map, PHLF has made the area residents feel that they

FIGURE 4.6 Mexican War Streets

are known and visible, rather than forgotten and lost.

In carrying out building rehabilitation in the Mexican War Streets, the Pittsburgh History and Landmarks Foundation moved away from the traditional and usually costly practices of restoring a building to an exact historic period; that is although uncovering and preserving architectural character and details were encouraged in renewing exterior facades, a costly restoration of the orignal exterior was not attempted. Further economies were recommended for the interior:

> Here are a few examples of corner-cutting to achieve minimal restorations.
>
> - Stud old interior walls and sheet with drywall rather than replastering.
> - Paint over old wallpaper if possible.
> - Scrape and paint old floors.
> - If a floor covering is required, use linoleum.
> - Use rubber stair treads, not carpet, on hall stairs.
> - If new bathroom plumbing is needed, do not tear up the old floor; lay the pipes over it and build a raised new floor on top.
> - Keep the existing sinks, bathtub, lights and other fixtures insofar as possible.
> - Paint woodwork; don't try to refinish it.
> - Have tenants help with the work, like painting.
> - Enlist federally funded Neighborhood Youth Corps youngsters to help.[9]

In this way PHLF was able to achieve a "minimal restoration" that made the interior neat and livable and renewed the exterior facade without extensive restoration or unnecessary modernization.

The success of preservation in the Mexican War Streets may have been due in part to their location adjacent to the historic Allegheny commons and near the Allegheny Center Mall, where another PHLF preservation effort was focused on the old Allegheny Post Office Building of 1894-1897. This beaux-arts post office, in the mall redevelopment area, had been scheduled for demolition after 1968. PHLF proposed instead that it be preserved and used as a museum of Pittsburgh and Allegheny County. After a public campaign, including petitions and public demonstration at the building, PHLF was able to convince the redevelopment authority to sell the building to the foundation. They paid $116,000 for the building and raised $750,000 in a public fund drive to be spent for restoration. The location of the building across from the Buhl Planetarium and the first Carnegie Library was entirely suited to its new use as a local history museum. PHLF now has its offices on the mezzanine floor. In the foundation brochures on the museum, an effort is made to link the Mexican War Streets preservation district to neighboring cultural attractions:

> The central part of Old Allegheny has always been a favorite place for an outing. We suggest the following: a visit to the Buhl Planetarium; then a walk next door to our museum; through the Commons to the conservatory-aviary, lake, and gardens, and finally, a stroll through the nearby Mexican War Streets, where Pittsburgh History and Landmarks Foundation has revived a handsome nineteenth-century neighborhood through its example in purchasing and restoring old houses. Visit Old Allegheny and come to the *lively landmark.*[10]

This linkage gives publicity to the preservation area and makes it more visible to the public.

An interesting and innovative sidelight of the museum has been the development of a sculpture court for artifacts, exterior and interior architectural ornaments and fittings retrieved by PHLF from demolished buildings since 1966. Although it is preferable not to have the buildings demolished, the sculpture court offers a way to save the most interesting fragments for the public and to increase public interest in preserving other buildings in the future.

The approach taken by PHLF on Liverpool Street and the Mexican War Streets has also been utilized in a third area of the city, Birmingham, on Pittsburgh's South Side. The area is a white working-class area, and PHLF has worked with the South Side Community Council and the South Side Chamber of Commerce to bring preservation to the community. This effort has been directed both at residences and commercial stores on Carson Street; it has emphasized self-help and "minimal restoration," with most of the work being done with private funds. While PHLF lobbied the city for public improvements in streets, trees, lighting, a private Birmingham

FIGURE 4.7 (above) Allegheny Post Office Building—Pittsburgh History and Landmarks Foundation office and local history museum; (below) Sculpture court

FIGURE 4.8   Carson Street, Birmingham district

Corporation was established to buy and restore commercial property, and the local American Institute of Architects chapter offered free architectural advice on restoration of buildings. These varied efforts from 1968 to 1970 were described by PHLF in the seventh issue of the *Stones of Pittsburgh* in a way intended to provide further incentive for the preservation effort among the residents of the area. The success of ideas such as "an area with a past has a future" and "a working-class Georgetown" in appealing to the residents of Birmingham suggests the essential stability of the community. To say that an old building with interesting architecture is valuable is a tentative statement. The owner of the building and his neighbors must believe it, and then invest time and money to realize the value. In Birmingham, the residents were able to accept this premise and to make the investment in time and money. In a slum, on the other hand, the residents will not usually accept it, and the investment of time and money will not be forthcoming. Indeed, for the slum dweller, concerned with basic livelihood and the threat of crime, this may be an accurate assessment of the value of preservation for him.

Added to the major elements of the Pittsburgh History and Landmarks Foundation program—community self-help, revolving fund, demonstration projects, advisory services, and public financing proposals—have been a number of the usual activities of a preservation organization. These have included the preservation of the Neill Log House, the marking of historic landmarks and buildings, publications, exhibits, tours, a survey of the historic architecture of Allegheny County, and acting as a preservation planning source for the city and for several businesses and churches. However, the main thrust of the PHLF program has been and continues to be the preservation of the inner-city neighborhood.

The areas preserved in Pittsburgh, when compared with the size of the entire city and the large number of buildings requiring rehabilitation, are small; nevertheless, PHLF has continued its programs and is expanding its attention to include new neighborhoods. In 1973 a new advisory service program was begun with funds provided by the National Endowment for the Arts and the Hillman Foundation. In one neighborhood, Allentown, this involved PHLF in a survey of the strengths and problems of the area. PHLF was invited to Allentown by the Hilltop Civic Improvement Association. After studying the area, PHLF held an exhibition to publicize its findings and published a report to be used in future work and planning for the neighborhood. This type of flexible service to inner-city neighborhoods is intended to be tailored to the needs of the area. PHLF can do a survey or become more deeply involved depending on the wishes of the people in the neighborhood.

The Pittsburgh approach has had a significance beyond its immediate impact on the city. This can be attributed to its groundbreaking preservation efforts in the inner city and also to Arthur Ziegler's excellent descriptions in *Historic Preservation in Inner City Areas* and in *Revolving Funds for Historic Preservation.* Both of these works are practical manuals that have acquainted preservationists beyond Pittsburgh with the creative work of the PHLF.

The account of preservation in Pittsburgh raises an interesting question—is historic preservation of an area a more effective route to neighborhood revitalization than rehabilitation pure and simple? In Pittsburgh, Action-Housing, Inc., a non profit organization working to rehabilitate inner-city neighborhoods, used a method and approach similar to PHLF, but without the historic preservation element. In one deteriorated black area, Bruston-Homewood, Action Housing held a number of planning and organization meetings with neighborhood residents. A great deal of enthusiasm was generated as a result, and many plans were made. However, money was slow in coming from public sources, and the enthusiasm soon turned to disappointment. The experience was similar to what happened to the PHLF in its effort on Liverpool Street. In both cases the shortage of public funds delayed rehabilitation, and in both self-help efforts were limited in scope because of the poverty of the residents. Nevertheless, there may have been one positive development as a result in Liverpool Street that did not occur in Bruston-Homewood. The residents of Liverpool Street, through the publicity and publications of PHLF, came to see their surroundings not simply as old and deteriorated, but instead as old and interesting in architecture and history. Even without extensive restoration, this made Liverpool Street a more attractive neighborhood for its residents and thus encouraged them in their efforts at neighborhood rehabilitation.

5. NEIGHBORHOOD PRESERVATION:
Stabilizing the Community

Neighborhoods that have undergone preservation, whether fostered by a preservation organization or generated spontaneously, seem to share certain characteristics. They are often historic, but this may not be the key factor; rather, it is that they provide a desired residential environment within or near a large city. In Boston, Beacon Hill met and continues to meet this need. When Beacon Hill became crowded and too expensive, preservation began in the Back Bay neighborhoods; and from there it has pushed on to the South End of Boston. Similarly, in Washington, D.C., Georgetown served this purpose. During World War II when housing in Washington was scarce, Alexandria was discovered, and now preservation has moved on to the Capitol Hill and Adams-Morgan neighborhoods. Today we are conscious of preservation and will usually try to ensure the process through community organization and historic district designation, but in the past this process often occurred without these added measures.

Beacon Hill, Boston

Beacon Hill was one of the first urban neighborhoods to undergo preservation. Although it was among the original historic districts— designated under state law in 1955 and expanded in 1958 and 1964— the attempt to protect the residential and historical character of Beacon Hill began much earlier with the formation of the Beacon Hill Civic Association (BHCA) in 1922. The BHCA worked to sustain community feeling for the area and to stop encroachments on its residential character by surrounding institutions or commercial establishments. This was at first achieved through zoning and then through the historic district with its architectural commission. The civic association helped see the historic district law through the Massachusetts legislature. In preparing the law, BHCA conducted a study of existing historic district legislation in other cities and also surveyed historic structures in the Beacon Hill area.[1] The association argued that the historic district designation would keep Beacon Hill from becoming a slum and linked this to the city's neighborhood conservation program.

Leaving aside the architectural operations of the historic district, which are similar to those we have already considered, there are several ways in which the BHCA has worked to preserve the neighborhood community on Beacon Hill. Newcomers to the neighborhood receive a "welcome folder" that contains general information about Beacon Hill and about the civic association, which they are invited to join. This orientation packet attempts to make the

FIGURE 5.1   Louisburg Square, Beacon Hill

FIGURE 5.2   Beacon Hill

newcomers aware that they will be living in a special neighborhood with architectural controls, to acquaint them with neighborhood facilities and local businesses, and to bring neighborhood problems to their attention. As a densely populated urban neighborhood, Beacon Hill has several problems that require continual attention: trash and litter control, dog control, illegal parking, noise, and residential burglaries. In each case the newcomer is given appropriate advice on trach pickup schedules, leash laws and curbing his dog, resident parking permits, keeping noise volume low, and various antiburglary measures from door locks to precautions to take when he may be out of town.

On the positive side, the newcomers are invited to participate in

the BHCA and work on any of the seventeen committees organized
by the association. They are also informed of other programs of the
association, such as window box gardening, recreation and cultural
activities, and tours of the district. The BHCA and other
neighborhood groups have their offices in the Hill House Community
Center, a former police station given to the community; various
programs for children, adolescents, and senior citizens are conducted
at the center.

Involving new residents in the community is one aspect of
neighborhood preservation; another aspect is maintenance of the
traditional neighborhood shopping area, in this case Charles Street.
Because the shops on Charles Street have not had enough local trade,
they have become increasingly unstable. In recent years, this problem
has received the combined attention of the BHCA, the Charles Street
Merchants Association, and the Boston Redevelopment Authority. A
planning report, with recommendations to resolve the problem, was
written in 1974.[2] As with the Vieux Carré, part of the problem is local
in nature, while other aspects result from the traffic and shoppers
from beyond the Beacon Hill area. The Charles Street report
identified the following problems: high rents, high rates of turnover
and vacancy, inadequate retail mix and poor space use, illegal
parking, and traffic congestion. The high rents and high rates of turnover on the street are related to the use of the area by specialty stores
(antique, youth culture, and trend shops). These enterprises tend to
displace neighborhood service stores; yet by their nature they are less
stable and offer less to the local community. The report suggests a
lower tax assessment by the city, based on a potential gross income
formula, would help to lower rents. It also suggests renovations of
facades, creation of interior shopping arcades and larger stores,
conversion of some retail space to residential use, and a coordinated
advertising campaign to promote the area. These measures are
intended to strengthen the retail base while discouraging the inflation
of rent levels. The improvement of the retail spaces and the
promotion of the area could certainly be achieved, but the
improvement of the retail mix and the deflation of rents is less likely
to occur.

Other recommendations in the report concern the street
environment and traffic. Street improvements, such as trees,
lighting, and sidewalk repair, are suggested as a public investment in

the area; these should be matched by facade improvements by private owners. The proposals for traffic improvements focus on increasing parking and parking turnover, instituting a minibus program to relieve the shortage of parking, and undertaking a traffic circulation study to analyze possible ways to reduce congestion. The street environment can be readily improved; the traffic and parking problems are more incorrigible.

The parking and traffic problem is not unrelated to the problem of high rents and poor retail mix. Beacon Hill residents do not usually drive to Charles Street, and they patronize, in the main, stores serving their local needs. Visitors and tourists, on the other hand, usually drive to the area and patronize specialty stores catering to their whims. Local residents make use of laundries, variety stores, drug stores, and markets that seldom attract visitors and tourists, and that cannot afford the high rents a specialty store can pay. The distribution of local service and specialty stores can be in balance; but on Charles Street during the brief "hippie invasion" of 1969, this balance was upset in favor of specialty stores, and local shoppers stopped coming to the street. The efforts of the BHCA and the redevelopment authority are attempts to redress the balance and thus sustain the usefulness of this commercial street to the Beacon Hill community.

In many ways, the shift in the commercial and social environment of Charles Street caused by the hippie invasion was a fortuitous occurrence; yet it reveals the difficulty that neighborhood preservation may have in dealing with unexpected changes, and the time-consuming effort that is required to get things back to "normal." Neighborhood preservationists, increasingly aware of this kind of problem, have attempted to gain greater control over economic and social factors that may influence their neighborhood. The BHCA has entered into planning discussions with several different institutional influences on or near Beacon Hill. For example, the West End Renewal Project, adjacent to the north side of Beacon Hill, will create a new shopping center in the area; the BHCA and the redevelopment authority have both worked to plan and control the impact of this new commercial center on existing commercial areas in Beacon Hill. Similarly, the BHCA has worked with Massachusetts General Hospital, across Cambridge Street from Beacon Hill, to limit hospital incursion on residential property in the area. And finally the BHCA has worked with Suffolk University, located on Beacon Hill, to plan for university expansion and student residence needs. Fortunately for the BHCA, the leaders of these institutions have been willing to consider neighborhood preservation in their planning.

Neighborhood preservation on Beacon Hill, without bringing in the problems of architectural preservation and control, is clearly a ✓ complex matter. The residents must be involved with the community and its problems, the local businesses must serve local needs, local residents must patronize them, and the major institutions in the area must recognize the needs of the community. Some of this can be planned out by the civic association, but a great deal depends upon the undefinable goodwill of those involved, and even then things can go awry.

Preservation has been an important factor in the life of Beacon Hill for several decades; the BHCA has an established and settled role in organizing and planning for the community. In contrast, there are many neighborhoods where preservation began only in the last decade. In these new areas, the major emphasis must be to establish the feasibility of neighborhood preservation and then to make it successful. One such neighborhood has been the Lafayette Square area in St. Louis where preservation first got underway in the late 1960s.

Lafayette Square, Saint Louis

The Lafayette Square neighborhood was fashionable in Saint Louis in the Victorian era, but slowly declined after the 1890s as newer areas replaced it. After World War II the thirty-acre Lafayette Square Park, a beautiful landscaped space, was neglected. Some of the large houses remained as family residences, but many became rooming houses or were divided into apartments. In large measure, Saint Louisans forgot about Lafayette Square, and it simply became a part of the deteriorated near South Side.

In the late 1960s, a small group of preservationists rediscovered the square and organized the Lafayette Square Restoration Committee. Several of them bought houses and restored them. In 1969 they began an annual house tour and in 1972 a neighborhood paper, the *Lafayette Square Meter*. To aid newcomers attracted to the square by publicity or word of mouth, the restoration committee published a list of available buildings with descriptions and set up a "one to one" committee of resident volunteers to give advice to those interested in buying and restoring a house in the neighborhood. Another committee handout described some of the things, such as plaster work, woodwork, plumbing, roof and guttering, cornices, to be considered by a prospective restorer in evaluating a house and recommended popular guides to restoration, such as *Buying and Renovating a House in the City,* by Stanforth and Stamm, or *Remodeling Old Houses without Destroying Their Character,* by Stephen. In this way newcomers were welcomed to the square and encouraged in the sometimes difficult task of restoration.

In carrying out their restoration, often on their own with a small budget and without the aid of an architect, the new residents had a continual stream of advice and examples from their fellow residents. These accounts of restoration in progress often appeared in the *Lafayette Square Meter* where they served as an antidote to the depression that might be experienced in contemplating what had to be done:

> All the rest of the work involved in fixing up a derelict house your-self runs pretty much in the same vein—moments of quiet desperation relieved by tremendous satisfactions. There are some real highs, like when you have finally made that big hole in your bedroom wall dis-appear without a trace. There are depressions too, though, when you begin to compute your cracked ceilings in units of acres rather than square feet. Wondering if you'll ever escape the dust, you tend to develop a rather elastic approach to life, in which the most bizarre things no longer seem strange. You begin to realize that you and most of your neighbors are becoming remarkable Mr. Pennypackers, living two different lives: one in the straight world of business and solid walls; the other in the lavender world of restoration.[3]

Residents gained a sense of communal accomplishment in reading and hearing about what others were doing.

At first, even buying a house on the square was difficult. The area, along with much of inner-city Saint Louis, was redlined and thus off-limits to lending institutions. House insurance was also unobtainable. The first nine houses purchased for restoration were sold on a cash and deed of trust arrangement between buyer and seller. One local savings-and-loan institution, after listening to the restoration

FIGURE 5.3 (*above*) Lafayette Square; (*below*) Visitors' Center display

committee, agreed to consider loans in the area, but other lenders did not believe the area could be restored. In 1972, the mayor of Saint Louis, at the request of the restoration committee, asked the lending institutions to consider loans in the Lafayette Square neighborhood. At the same time the city nominated the area to the National Register of Historic Places and designated it as Saint Louis's first historic district. After that, more lenders were willing to make loans in the neighborhood, but a high down payment was often required. Home insurance also became more readily available.

In 1974, the city allocated funds for work to be done in the park and for the restoration of the little police station building in the park. The interior was refurbished by the restoration committee for use as a visitor's center and for displays related to the history of Lafayette Square.

The resurgence of Lafayette Square has been slow. The restoration committee has had the support of the Landmarks Association of Saint Louis, of Heritage/Saint Louis, and of the Saint Louis chapter of the AIA. The AIA chapter undertook an architectural survey of the area in 1969, and the landmarks association published it as part of a booklet on the history of the square.

As an urban neighborhood, Lafayette Square has not suffered from the kinds of pressures at work on Beacon Hill. Although the crime rate was very high in Lafayette Square prior to restoration, it has steadily declined as the transient rooming house population has been replaced by young professional families. Commercial areas adjacent to the square neighborhood have experienced some entry of new business; however, there were vacant locations to accommodate them and as a result local service businesses have not been affected. Traffic has not been a problem either. Although a proposed highway connection was at one point planned through part of the historic district, it was opposed by the restoration committee and its allies and successfully rerouted in 1975. There is some hope that not even the alternate route will be constructed.

Lafayette Square has not been the only Saint Louis neighborhood in which preservationists have been active. Preservation has also been attempted in the Soulard neighborhood and in the Central West End. Soulard was a German and Bohemian working-class area of small houses built after 1840. Several breweries, including what has become the Anheuser-Busch complex, were located there. Soulard

FIGURE 5.4   Soulard streetscape

was first proposed as an historic district in 1969 and was nominated to the National Register of Historic Places in 1972. Prior to 1970, the district had not suffered many demolitions, but the rate has subsequently increased as houses have been abandoned. The Soulard Neighborhood Association has attempted to carry out preservation without changing the working-class composition of the area; however, shortage of funds has limited the group's preservation work. At the same time Soulard has not attracted new residents with the money or know-how to support preservation in the area. The prospect is bleak and unfortunate, as the architectural resources of Soulard provide a unique picture of Saint Louis in the mid-nineteenth century. The situation could change quickly if the Anheuser-Busch company made a commitment to restoration of the area. As it is, thousands of tourists visit the brewery, and an Historic Soulard to visit would be a natural adjunct to that attraction. However, although it has manufactured Historic Saint Louis at its Busch Gardens amusement parks and built the Old World next to Williamsburg, Anheuser-Busch has shown little interest in restoring Soulard.

In contrast to Soulard, the Central West End is an area of large houses on private streets. The Central West End Association, established in 1958, is an umbrella organization for neighborhood groups. The main purpose of the association is to promote a positive attitude about the area through its various programs from preservation to crime abatement. The Central West End was not deteriorated; thus the programs of the association are intended to maintain and enhance the existing stability of the area and to break the pattern of white flight to suburbia that was established in Saint Louis in the 1960s. The substantial houses and the private streets of the area have facilitated the efforts of the association: crime rates have declined, local businesses have remained in the area, and lending institutions have seen a favorable picture of increasing property values. The association has proposed an historic district for the area, which may be another way of ensuring stability; but its main efforts are in maintaining the image of the area and attracting new businesses and residents.

Considering the Saint Louis pattern of white flight to the suburbs, the restoration of Lafayette Square has clearly been an exception. Aside from the Central West End, which has held its own, central Saint Louis has experienced a pattern of deterioration and demolition in most of its neighborhoods. The example set in the restoration of Lafayette Square has had citywide impact, and other neighborhoods have started to follow suit. Some areas, like the affluent and well-maintained Compton Hill neighborhood, will undoubtedly be successful; other areas, like the partially deteriorated or demolished Hyde Park and the Old Water Tower neighborhoods, will have greater difficulties. In Lafayette Square, the success of restoration has depended upon an influx of committed young preservationists who have been able to substitute inspiration and personal work for money and professional restoration. This kind of an influx cannot be confidently assumed in other neighborhoods. In many Eastern and Midwestern cities, the number of neighborhoods that have the architectural potential for historic preservation far exceeds the number of preservationists to undertake the effort or the funds available to pay for the work. However, rising costs and demand for houses may force many members of the baby-boom generation to buy houses in older neighborhoods. Some of them may make a virtue of necessity by becoming preservationists.

Neighborhood Improvement in Seattle

The examples of neighborhood preservation we have examined thus far occurred largely without the aid of public funds; this need not be the case. Public funds, such as community development block grants, can be used effectively for neighborhood preservation. An exceptional program carried out in Seattle shows how public funds might assist neighborhood renovation. The Seattle program began with a citywide study of neighborhoods undertaken by the Department of Community Development in the 1960s. The study found twenty critical neighborhoods that required improvements to ensure their stability. A $12 million Forward Thrust bond issue was proposed and approved by city voters in 1968; the funds were divided among the twenty neighborhoods and were to be used for street-related public improvement. These included street and sidewalk repairs, new paving and lighting, underground wiring, bike lanes, traffic diverters, drain and sewer improvements, and tree planting. In fact, as we shall see, the program was to cover zoning, housing rehabilitation, neighborhood services, and other aspects of community development as well as street improvements.

The provisions of the Forward Thrust ordinance were carried out through the Office of Neighborhood Planning, with a planner assigned to each neighborhood. The methods of involving the neighborhood community in planning the allocation of the improvement funds are most revealing for anyone attempting a preservation program. The planner began by contacting neighborhood groups and organizations and asking them to identify neighborhood problems and desired improvements. At the same time, an announcement was sent to all neighborhood residents of a public meeting to discuss the possible uses of the improvement funds. Notices were also posted around the area. At the meeting, run by neighborhood residents, the planner explained the program. Suggestions for projects were then solicited from the audience, followed by the election of a neighborhood improvement committee to work with the planning office. In this way members of the community were involved in identifying their problems and planning their solution. From this involvement came a deeper commitment to the neighborhood.

Taking the problems suggested by the neighborhood, the planner proceeded in several directions. Some of the problems could be dealt with through the street improvement funds; these were studied for feasibility and cost. Other problems were a result of zoning or housing deterioration. In these cases the planner examined the problem and recommended zoning changes or low-interest housing rehabilitation loans. Another set of problems, found in the poorest neighborhoods, concerned jobs, crime, and welfare services. With these, the planner examined the issues and contacted relevant city agencies with recommendations on how to improve services to the residents. In this way, as the program evolved, the planner developed a complex description of and plan for the neighborhood. This plan was more comprehensive than the immediate street improvements and provided a basis for later actions by the city and by the neighborhood organizations.

When the cost and feasibility of the various street improvement proposals had been determined, all of the proposals and costs were presented to neighborhood residents for their vote. They received a mailed announcement of time and place for the polling and a description of the projects proposed. Projects were selected based on the outcome of the vote, and the work was then carried out by the city.

While the street improvements were being carried out, the Office of Neighborhood Planning issued a foldout Neighborhood Improvement Plan brochure that was mailed to the area residents. The plan summarized information about the area, including descriptions of land use, circulation, parks, and public facilities, and presented recommendations and projects in each area. The information was also represented on a large multicolor map of the area. Through this brochure and map, residents who had not participated in the planning process were once again acquainted with the projects and recommendations.

The Seattle neighborhood program adhered to a very open and democratic planning procedure; yet even after mailings and announcements, usually only 1 percent of the residents actively participated in the meetings, and usually less than 5 percent were involved in the voting. Furthermore, the planners found that although this planning approach was effective in middle- and lower-middle-income areas, it was very difficult to get sustained participation in poor areas. They also found that although the input of

public funds in middle- and lower-middle-income areas was enhanced by community organization and various self-help actions, in
the poorer areas the input of funds was met by requests for further
services in problem areas beyond the scope of the neighborhood
planning office. As result of these responses, the neighborhood
improvement program and plan tended to be more effective and
successful in the middle- and lower-middle-income areas.

In terms of neighborhood preservation and conservation, Seattle's
program of public investment in street improvements was often
matched by private investment in housing restoration. This was
clearly the result in the Stevens neighborhood on Capitol Hill. This
single-family residential area had begun to improve prior to the
neighborhood program, but there were several problems with traffic
using residential streets, zoning that threatened higher-density
development, and the absence of a community center. Through the
street improvement projects, a system of traffic diverters was placed
in the residential streets to discourage the use of those streets by
through traffic; other street projects were directed toward
improving traffic flow on main arteries through the area. The
neighborhood plan recommended that several areas in the Stevens
neighborhood be down-zoned to prevent high-density apartment
buildings from replacing the single-family dwellings. The plan also
recommended the extension of the city Neighborhood Housing
Rehabilitation Program to include the Stevens area, thus making
low-interest loans available for improvement of properties. Finally,
the plan proposed the use and renovation of a city-owned building for
a community center.

In Stevens, at least, the existence of an overlap of the
neighborhood improvement program with historic preservation is
clear. The Capitol Hill area was one of the first two areas selected for
an historic survey and urban design inventory by the recently established Historic Seattle Preservation and Development Authority,
a city-sponsored public corporation. The survey, like the planning
process we have just examined, is a means of public education as well
as a means of gathering information. The surveyors are volunteers,
enlisted with the aid of the community councils. They are given a
preliminary lecture by the architectural consultants of the survey, an
information packet describing various architectural styles and

FIGURE 5.5 Stevens—Capitol Hill neighborhood

characteristic details, and survey forms. The volunteers are told to be inclusive rather than exclusive, noting and photographing all the buildings they feel to be significant. Although the architectural consultants may later, in compiling the results, weed out a few of the volunteer selections, the volunteers' interest in the architecture of the neighborhood has been aroused. The results of the survey are later published as a foldout brochure. In fostering neighborhood preservation the Historic Seattle Preservation and Development Authority has chosen to start with a survey; later it may take a more active role using the $600,000 revolving fund with which it was entrusted by the city. On the other hand, the Office of Neighborhood Planning of the Department of Community Development seeks to foster preservation through zoning and street improvements. Architectural style appeals to some residents, zoning and street improvements to others. The outcomes of both activities are complementary as they enhance community image and organization and foster preservation.

Historic Hill District, Saint Paul

The neighborhood improvement program in Seattle, although it illustrates a community involvement preservation process aided by municipal funds, has not emphasized historic aspects of the areas. Recently, in Saint Paul, Minnesota, an ambitious neighborhood preservation program has evolved through the efforts of several community groups that combines community involvement and historic preservation. This program, working in the Historic Hill District of the city, illustrates effective techniques developed to achieve architectural preservation through community efforts within the neighborhood. The participants have described the full scope of this effort in an interesting report, *Building the Future from Our Past.* [4]

The Historic Hill District of Saint Paul is composed of several neighborhoods with somewhat different histories. The district as a whole had been suffering from deterioration and blight spreading southward from a northern boundary formed by Interstate 94. This highway runs through a black community and has displaced people to both sides of its path. In 1953 Saint Paul initiated a Summit–University Renewal Project on this northern section of the Historic Hill District. The resulting demolitions, vacant spaces, and out-of-place modern apartment units did little to resolve the social problems of this northern area, and the negative image of the renewal project gradually affected areas to its south.

The houses of the Historic Hill District were built between the 1880s and the 1920s for the wealthy and middle-class residents. Since parts of the hill had been fashionable neighborhoods, the houses that remain are large, architecturally interesting, and well constructed. During and after the Depression, the area slowly changed as larger houses were subdivided for apartments and as many families moved to the suburbs. Traffic congestion and road widening on the hill in the 1950s further detracted from the area. The pattern of change is a familiar one; however, several areas of the hill remained as single-family middle-class neighborhoods, and these became the nuclei in the effort for preservation that began in the late 1960s.

The first organization to work for improvement of the image of the area and to oppose further goverment-sponsored renewal via demolition was the Summit Hill Association formed in 1967. The neighborhood this organization represented comprised the southern portion of the district, was predominantly white and middle class, and had suffered little blight. The Summit Hill Association was thus primarily protective in its orientation, trying to prevent the spread of blight into its area. The example of the Summit Hill Association was followed by the Lexington/Hamline Community Council, which formed in 1968; the Ramsey Hill Association, in 1972; and the Portland Avenue Association, in 1974. The last two neighborhoods, occupying the center and eastern portions of the hill, have experienced more deterioration and blight, and have been the main areas in which house restorations have been taking place.

Two factors have facilitated preservation in the hill district. The first was the designation of the Historic Hill District by the state legislature in 1973, which has been a strong, positive image-building factor for all of the neighborhoods. The second was the formation in 1974 of Old Town Restorations, Inc., a nonprofit umbrella group. This group has carried out the preservation planning for the Historic Hill District and has formulated a variety of new concepts and policies that have fostered preservation and influenced the entire "Back to the City" movement.

Old Town Restorations began preservation planning for the hill district in March 1974 with a small grant from the Minnesota State Arts Council. In June 1974 they received a $50,000 grant from the National Endowment for the Arts under the City Options Program, which the Northwest Area Foundation later matched with $70,000 to extend the planning program for another year. The Old Town group set out to develop a resident-controlled community-based planning program that would result in neighborhood and historic preservation. In this they sought to avoid the city-imposed and planned urban renewal procedure of the 1950s and 1960s.

Stressing communication and resident involvement, the planning process began with four public meetings sponsored by Old Town Restorations and the neighborhood associations at four different churches in the district. Each took a different area of concern: land use, design and architecture, community services, and traffic and circulation. Meeting announcements were distributed in the community and published in community newspapers. Over 100 people attended each meeting out of a district population of 29,000; nevertheless, this was sufficient to reflect the various social and economic viewpoints of the residents.

Four Citizen Planning Committees were set up, one for each area of concern, to analyze the issues raised at the public meetings. The committees publicized their work in mailed progress reports and newspaper articles, and they received advice from a team of professionals in architecture, planning, and history, and from community organizations working with Old Town Restorations. After a series of meetings, these committees filed reports that then comprised a preliminary plan. The reports were reviewed at a public meeting so that residents could make further comments. The University of Minnesota's Center for Urban and Regional Affairs and the School of Architecture, the Minnesota Historical Society, the Housing and Redevelopment Authority, the City Planning Department, and the Minnesota Society of Architects assisted by providing professional evaluation of the planning and proposals.

The resulting plan first considered the history, design, and architecture of the hill district. It reviewed the social and historical development of the area from the initial settlement of Saint Paul in the 1850s to the present demographic profile. It also presented a parallel discussion of the architectural styles that were used in the district. The plan made the information available to the residents to establish a connection between them and the architectural tradition of the hill. In turn this would reinforce their interest in the community and their effort to preserve its buildings.

The second area of concern was land use: residential, commercial, institutional, recreational, and vacant. This supplemented the architectural inventory with a physical amenities inventory, a parks and recreation inventory, a microclimate study, and a visual imagery study. The last was concerned with significant or "imageable" aspects of the hill district such as vistas, paths, edges, nodes, landmarks, and gateways. The technique used, adopted from Kevin Lynch's *The Image of the City,* helps to identify aspects of the cityscape that together make up the identity of an area. The microclimate study examined the relationship of landscape to climate in producing a comfortable or uncomfortable environment for humans. In the hill district trees and other vegetation tend to moderate both winter winds and summer heat, whereas their replacement with parking lots has the opposite effect.

Taking the various inventories and surveys together, the planning team was able to pinpoint land use problems on the hill. For example, deteriorating areas and areas requiring commercial redevelopment were identified; areas lacking sufficient park space or other amenities became apparent; areas needing more trees were noted; and areas where imageability could be improved, at gateways and along commercial strips, became visible. Obviously, Old Town Restorations and the neighborhood associations could not hope to correct all of these; the intent of the planning analysis and report was rather to provide information and guidelines that the preservation groups could use in negotiating with relevant city departments, private institutions, commercial firms, or landowners.

To illustrate solutions the plan included a prototype residential block study and a commercial block study. For the residential block, which had both vacant spaces and two out-of-character houses, the study suggested single or multifamily in-fill housing of modern style and appropriate scale and setback, and relocation of old houses that would have been demolished from other areas. Old trees and lighting and old houses in the process of restoration provided an established architectural unity for the block; in-fill housing and replacement of out-of-character houses would remove nonharmonious elements. When once the character of an area is recognized, or controlled in an historic district, it is usually possible to influence the design of new structures. However, it is another matter to remove nonharmonious buildings and probably this should not be expected.

The commercial study considered a block with three unrelated types of buildings; a three-story bayfront set, a one-story commercial storefront set, and a single-story modern building with a curvilinear roof. These buildings were not architecturally compatible. In order to create an architecturally unified block, the study suggested tying the first two sets of buildings together through a unified renovation of the street-level facades and uniform graphics. It also suggested replacing the curvilinear roof on the last building with a flat roof, or replacing the building as a whole with entirely new and compatible buildings. Once again, it is reasonable to propose facade renovations, harmonious graphics, and signs in an historic area, but the replacement of entire buildings is usually not economically feasible.

The third area of concern in the planning report was traffic and circulation in, through, and around the district neighborhoods. Practically, this meant automobile traffic and proposed alternatives to the automobiles. Located near the downtown, the hill district is subject to crosstown traffic. Fortunately, the freeway along the northern border of the district takes a large volume of this traffic, and two of the crosstown routes in the district are designated as parkways and thus closed to commercial traffic. The study proposes that other crosstown routes in the district be designated as parkways as a way of removing more undesirable traffic. The parkway restriction on commercial vehicles could be a useful tool for preservationists and might be considered for use in other historic areas.

Aside from the crosstown routes, most traffic on the hill is local and presents only the usual parking problems; adverse consequences result from demolition of buildings for parking lots and from the microclimate created by these lots. To reduce the need for parking lots and for local automobile traffic, the planners have suggested several transportation alternatives. The first would involve the upgrading of pedestrian walkways, by widening, addition of benches and ramps, better lighting, and tree planting for shade. These are practical improvements that could be carried out by the city, but they address only part of the problem. To induce people to walk, rather than use their cars, it is necessary to revitalize local shops within walking distance. In the district, and similar areas elsewhere, local shops have closed after losing trade to automobile-oriented markets and shopping centers. Reversing this trend is a precondition for pedestrian improvements to succeed.

The second alternative suggestion concerns the establishment of bicycle routes in the hill district to provide bicycle riders with a way free of both cars and pedestrians, and thus encourage bicycle use. The idea is popular with urban dwellers in general and with planners, but the implementation of bike paths has not been universally acclaimed. In the Seattle Neighborhood Improvement Program, bike paths were a popular improvement suggested and voted for by the residents; however, when the residents along the proposed routes were surveyed, they often opposed the bikepaths, which then were not put in. The residents did not wish to sacrifice their parking or their privacy to the pathways. In Los Angeles, similar problems have arisen along proposed routes, and merchants have argued against the loss of customer parking. In any case, the largest percentage of bicycle use is for pleasure and has not noticeably reduced the number of local automobile trips for shopping in our cities. Few people drive for pleasure in their own neighborhoods.

A final transportation alternative suggested in the plan is the revival of the trolley system that once served the hill district and connected it to the downtown area. Considering the investment involved in carrying out this suggestion and the relatively small area of the city that would benefit, this idea will probably not be realized. Efforts to control traffic in and through an historic area always present difficult problems.

The fourth area of concern in the plan was community services and facilities in the hill district. As an area deteriorates there is usually a marked deterioration in services and facilities. To rehabilitate and preserve the area this trend must be reversed. These facilities cover a broad range of social needs including schools, health facilities, local commercial shops, community centers, police facilities, recreational facilities, and churches. In the older neighborhoods they are often scarce or absent. To further complicate the picture, halfway houses and other residential treatment facilities for mental patients or parolees are often located in older areas where facilities are inexpensive and there is no great objection from the residents. Though they need not, such facilities for transients can hasten the deterioration of a neighborhood by disrupting the social fabric. The task, then, for preservationists is twofold: to encourage the rehabilitation of needed community service facilities, and to discourage the placement of too many detrimental facilities in the area.

In the use of some neighborhood facilities preservationists can be effective as individuals and as groups in causing a positive change. Parental involvement with the local schools can change the educational environment. Preservation groups have often joined with other community organizations in establishing a community center. Relations between police and community as well as police activities to prevent crime can often be improved through meetings between local officers and neighborhood residents. New and old businesses can be encouraged through resident patronage and the attention of neighborhood groups. Church involvement in the community can be requested by neighborhood groups and suggested by individual parishioners.

On the other hand, positive change often depends upon preservation groups influencing the appropriate city or institutional agency. Improvements in parks, school funding, police staffing, and health care facilities are often dependent upon city policy toward the area. An equitable citywide distribution of residential treatment facilities is also dependent on city policy. In these service areas the neighborhood associations must convince the city that private investment in the neighborhood depends upon, and should be matched by, public investment.

Private preservation resources are sufficient for the task of rehabilitating most houses and some commercial buildings; they are sufficient for the creation of historic building inventories; they are sufficient for the formation of community organizations; but in the broader areas of land use control, transportation, and community services, preservationists must appeal for the aid and support of their city government. The Historic Hill District planning program recognizes this; its appeal is directed both to the neighborhood resident and to the city agencies. The future success and expansion of preservation in the hill district depend upon the cooperation of both groups.

Ethnic Neighborhood Preservation: German Village and Little Italy

In our discussion of neighborhood preservation, we have assumed that preservation came about because of the attraction of the historic architecture, or because the area became a desirable place to live as a result of its location or reasonable real estate costs. An additional reason for preservation must be recognized: the desire by an ethnic, religious, or racial group to preserve or restore an area of initial immigrant settlement. This motivation is not particularly recent in origin. Several historic houses have been preserved by descendants of the family that lived as pioneers in the family homestead, and several religious villages or settlements have been restored by modern adherents of the respective religion. One thinks of the Fairbanks, Aldens, and Howlands family homesteads in New England, the Shaker Village in Pennsylvania, or the Mormon restorations in Nauvoo, Illinois, as examples of this kind of preservation.

In urban areas, a similar motivation can lead to the preservation of neighborhoods of initial settlement, such as the German Village in

Columbus, Ohio, and the Little Italy section of Manhattan in New York City. The German Village was an area of initial settlement for German immigrants to America in the nineteenth century. Modest houses were built by the immigrants, businesses were started, and German cultural life was continued through the use of the German language, through German newspapers, and through community organizations such as the Columbus Mannerchor, the Germanic Singing and Sports Society, and other ethnic associations. The community thrived until the First World War when popular anti-German sentiments hurt German-owned businesses and placed a stigma on German cultural activities. Despite the respite that followed the war, second and third generation German-Americans left the German Village for other areas of Columbus where they would not be subject to hostility. The village area slowly declined as businesses closed and families left. Continuing examples of German cultural life in the village once again met with suspicion during the Second World War, and this completed the dissolution of Columbus's German community. After World War II, the village area became a slum and a likely candidate for urban clearance.

The condition of the village remained unchanged until the organization of the German Village Society in 1960. Formed by descendants of the immigrants, the society proposed the restoration and preservation of the village. Several members of the society moved back into the area and began restorations; in the meantime, an annual *"Haus und Garten"* Tour was initiated. In 1963 the society persuaded the Columbus City Council to designate the village an

FIGURE 5.6 (*left* and *below*) German Village

historic area, and a German Village Commission was set up to regulate the architectural restorations and ensure historic appropriateness. The society purchased and restored one building for its offices and for use as an information center. Beyond that it depended upon publicity and encouragement to bring about restoration of the area and did not itself buy or sell buildings. The restoration example set by members of the society was followed by many old residents who moved back to the village, and this in turn attracted other people, not necessarily of German ancestry, who liked the old world ambience that was again emerging in the village.

In 1968 a German Village Business Association was formed to promote new business and tourism in the area. The association has since then been active in raising funds for brick paving and gaslights that may need repair, and it has assisted the adaptive commercial use of several large buildings in the village. The German Village Society has extended its activities with a "Backyards-by-Candlelight Tour," "Christmas in German Village" festivities, and a monthly newsletter, the *German Village News.* Without public funds or a private revolving fund, the village has been successfully restored as a thriving and stable community. This achievement reflects the interest of many Columbus residents in their German ancestry and heritage, and it reflects the attractiveness of the village with its modest houses and gardens so well suited to contemporary uses and tastes. The successful example set by the German Village in Columbus has inspired similar attempts at preservation in German areas of other cities, specifically in the Over-the-Rhine section of Cincinnati and the Soulard neighborhood of Saint Louis. However, these have not yet been as successful.

Another example of preservation in an ethnic neighborhood has been evident recently in the Little Italy neighborhood of Lower Manhattan. This area of four- and five-story buildings with small shops and restaurants at street level, adjacent to the Bowery, Chinatown, and the Lower East Side, became a place of initial settlement for Italian immigrants at the turn of the century. Over the years, thriving Italian groceries, bakeries, porkshops, restaurants, and cafes were established in the neighborhood. Even after many second- and third-generaion Italians moved away to better houses in the suburbs, they continued to return to Little Italy for these special services. The availability of Italian food and merchandise has also

FIGURE 5.7 Little Italy

made the area a tourist attraction.

Although Italian commerce has remained active in the neighborhood, the Italian population has slowly declined as young families have moved away from the tenement apartments above the shops and restaurants. Increasingly, the remaining Italian residents have been the elderly and poor; not enough young Italians have remained to replenish the community. At the same time, the increasing population of adjacent Chinatown, looking for apartment and storefront space, has begun to cross Canal Street into the Little Italy neighborhood.

Recognizing the need to promote and strengthen their Italian community, several neighborhood leaders organized in 1974 the Little Italy Restoration Association (LIRA). Several of the organizers had been active in the Neighborhood Council to Combat Poverty started in 1968, and LIRA was an outgrowth of that council. After studying the problems of the neighborhood, LIRA focused on several needs: new housing and housing rehabilitation, a community center, park improvements, pedestrianization of certain commercial areas and other street improvements, and improvements of health care and social services.

Answers and solutions to these needs are in the planning stage, but certain actions have been taken. Neighborhood residents lobbied against the construction of a new school on the site of old P.S. 21 until new middle-income housing was included along with the school. LIRA and other area groups feel that the new school will mainly serve Chinese youngsters, as the Italian children usually attend parochial school. They also feel that Little Italy needs new housing to attract young families back to the neighborhood. Proposals for upgrading existing housing are also intended to attract the young to the area. LIRA has proposed the conversion of the empty old Police Headquarters, a large beaux-arts building, into an Italian-American Cultural Center. Because of the shortage of city funds and the size of the building, this proposal may not be realized. However, the building has been recommended for landmark designation, and the city is studying the cultural center proposal. Park improvement plans have focused on De Salvio Park, the only park in the neighborhood; funds for rehabilitation were allocated by the city in 1975. LIRA has also encouraged residents to carry out flower and tree planting on their streets.

In the pedestrianization and street improvements area, LIRA has been successful in closing Mulberry Street in the evening hours and in having cafe tables placed on the sidewalks along with festive red, white, and green decorations. This *"pedonalizzazione,* a traditional Italian approach to creation of networks of malls and tiny piazzas,"[5] reinforces the Italian character of the neighborhood and complements the gold lettering and window displays of the Italian shops. The new ambience has drawn citywide attention to Little Italy and has attracted more visitors.

The work of LIRA has been reported to the community in a journal, *Risorgimento*, written by LIRA members. As the traditional center of New York's Italian community and the focus of numerous community celebrations and religious festivals, Little Italy has a strong existing sense of community to work with in carrying out preservation.

Preservation in the German Village and in Little Italy can serve as examples for other ethnic neighborhoods. In both cases, the emphasis is on reviving or maintaining the ethnic culture as well as on the restoration of the neighborhood buildings and surroundings. In the German Village, the houses are architecturally interesting and, having been built by the immigrants, form a natural element in the revival of the ethnic heritage of the neighborhood. But the revival is also reflected in the orchestra concerts in Schiller Park, in the German food at Schmidt's Sausage Haus, and in the German clothing sold in some of the village stores. In Little Italy the tenement buildings are not for the most part architecturally unique; the small walk-up apartments do of course suggest the living conditions experienced by the immigrants, but there is little that is attractive in preserving blocks of tenements. Thus in Little Italy, rehabilitation of the buildings has taken precedence over their restoration, and architectural interest has focused instead on the street-level stores and restaurants, the store windows, and street furniture, which convey the uniquely Italian character of the area.

Opportunities for preservation in ethnic neighborhoods exist in many cities in the Northeast and the West; offhand, one thinks of the Italian community in South Philadelphia, the Polish community of Chicago, or the Chinatowns of New York or San Francisco. We should expect that cultural preservation in ethnic neighborhoods will not always focus on building restoration. The ethnic ambience may depend on other design aspects of the neighborhood, and it will be these aspects that the ethnic community will seek to restore and preserve. As members of the ethnic community will be most sensitive to what is compatible with their culture, they must be depended upon to direct preservation in their neighborhoods. On the other hand, members of an ethnic community may not always be sensitive to the historic ambience of their neighborhood, and they may seek the assistance of preservationists to gain this sensitivity.

6. TOWN AND SMALL CITY PRESERVATION:
Comprehensive Preservation Planning

In the field of preservation, there are several cases that best exemplify the problems and approaches developed under the conditions prevailing in towns or small cities. The separation of town preservation from other kinds of preservation is to some extent artificial, as the techniques used are not so different from those applied in large cities. Nevertheless, because many of the preservation problems in towns result either from the local lack of sensitivity to preservation or from the town's proximity to a metropolis, preservationists have adopted environmental and growth policies that are often not needed by preservation groups in large cities.

The first problem faced by preservationists in towns and small cities has been the frequent neglect and ignorance displayed toward historic architecture by the townsfolk. To a certain extent this neglect has abated in recent years, but before that the usual small town attitude favored new buildings or the remodeling of old ones. Often in impoverished small towns, the oldest commercial buildings were abandoned, or used only at the street level, with the upper floors closed off. Residences fared better, but were often neglected by their poor inhabitants. As towns were depopulated after the Second World War, many houses were abandoned and boarded up. Public buildings, courthouses or city halls slowly deteriorated and were often replaced by simpler and smaller modern buildings. Old railroad stations received the same treatment.

The revival of small towns has been a gradual and at first unnoticed occurrence. Beginning in the 1960s, and in some cases earlier, some residents of large cities began to look for places of residence and work

149

free of urban congestion and pollution. They often found such havens in small towns. These newcomers to the small town frequently brought with them an urban sophistication and appreciation for the virtues of small town living that was lacking in the original residents of the town, and it was usually the newcomers who led the way to preservation.

Jacksonville, Oregon: Restoration

This process can be seen clearly in the course of preservation in Jacksonville, Oregon, a small town of 1,600 people.[1] Founded during the gold rush of the 1850s in southern Oregon, Jacksonville had thrived while the mines lasted, but then declined when the railroad bypassed the town. However, it continued to serve as the county seat until 1928 when the courthouse was moved to the neighboring city of Medford. After that, little remained to prevent further decline, and by the 1950s it was used by the neighboring cities as a settlement area for local welfare recipients because of the low rents.

Despite the economic and social condition of Jacksonville, it contained a significant collection of nineteenth-century brick and frame buildings. Although this was overlooked by most of the townspeople, it was not missed by a few outsiders and by members of the Southern Oregon Historical Society located in the Old Courthouse. When in the early 1960s a four-lane highway was proposed to cut through the town, the townspeople opposed and stopped it. Recognition of the historical interest of the town was a factor in resisting the highway. After this battle, preservation began slowly through the efforts of private individuals and private businesses. Robertson Collins, a preservationist and president of a local company, bought and restored a house in the town. He also bought and began to restore several of the old brick commercial buildings. With some friends who were also beginning to take an interest in Jacksonville, Collins convinced the U.S. National Bank of Portland to put a branch office planned for the town into the 1884 United States Hotel instead of a new building. The hotel building was faithfully restored with the ground floor as a nineteenth-century bank. The branch opening was the occasion for a three-day celebration that received publicity throughout the area.

After the positive reception given to the restoration of the hotel

FIGURE 6.1 *(above)* Jacksonville; *(below left)* United States Hotel

building, officers of the Pacific Power and Light Company decided to restore an early electric transformer station in Jacksonville as a branch office. It was later used as a tourist information center and has now been given to the historical society for use as an electrical museum. Local preservationists were later successful in persuading both the post office and the telephone company to utilize brick facing and an appropriate scale on new buildings they were constructing in the commercial area of the town.

Preservationists in Jacksonville had thought that the publicity given to the hotel and the restoration of houses and commercial buildings would lead the local townspeople to change their attitude toward their old houses and stores. Instead the publicity that preservation efforts received attracted new people to the town who were sympathetic to its historic and architectural village atmosphere. They bought and restored houses, and several antique shops opened in the old brick commercial buildings. Further attention was called to the town when it was used as the set for a western movie, and the number of tourists visiting Jacksonville increased annually.

Most of the town was placed on the National Register of Historic Places in 1967 in preparation for a model cities program to restore the town, but the program was never carried out because of objections from the city council, which did not want federal urban renewal regulations to intrude on local self-government. Some of the organizational aspects of preservation have been handled through the historical society, and at present the city has established a design review board for the nine-block downtown area. However, the course of preservation in the town has been mainly determined by the activities of private individuals and by the newcomers and businesses attracted by the publicity given to the town.

Socially, Jacksonville has gone from a poor and deteriorated town in the 1950s to a fashionable and restored historic town in the 1970s. Many of the new residents commute daily across the short distance of farmland that separates Jacksonville from Medford. In this, Jacksonville has not only been restored, but has become a village suburb of the neighboring city. As Jacksonville is restored and stabilized, the preservationists have begun to consider ways to protect the greenbelt that separates the town from Medford. This flat farmland is suited to development, and the new social prominence of Jacksonville has created a demand for housing in the vicinity that would make new development successful. The city council has favored development and has approved a trailer park and a supermarket of modern design. However, both add little to the historic character of the town. The very success of preservation has created this problem and has naturally led preservationists away from their immediate concern with the town and its buildings toward a more comprehensive concern with the environmental setting of the town and its pattern of future growth. In practical terms, this means they have had to be concerned with plans to improve the sewer system in the Medford-Jacksonville area, as the current system will not support further residential development. Clearly, the effort to preserve an historic town may lead preservationists rather far from their initial concerns.

Annapolis: Preservation and Conservation

Jacksonville illustrates many of the aspects of preservation in small towns; however, it is not an elaborate example. For a more complicated picture of the circumstances and conditions that influence preservation work in a small town we may look to Annapolis, Maryland. Nationally well-known as the site of the U.S. Naval Academy, Annapolis is also the state capital of Maryland. Architecturally, it has a good number of buildings from before the time of the Revolution through the early nineteenth-century; but aside from obvious landmark buildings such as the State House and Saint Anne's Church, these cultural assets were largely ignored until the strenuous efforts of Historic Annapolis, Inc., in the last two decades made the case for preservation.

In the 1950s most Annapolis residents thought their town was old and obsolete, and its historic architecture was obscured by neglect, shop signs, and modern improvements. There was little tourism, and the economic life of the town rested on the naval academy, the state government, and Saint John's College. Socially and culturally, Annapolis was a provincial backwater when compared with the sophistication of Baltimore and Washington.

In 1952 a few historically minded residents and some newcomers to the town organized Historic Annapolis, Inc. From the beginning, they intended to preserve the cityscape and landscape of the old town. Their first effort was the purchase of the Shiplap House in

FIGURE 6.2 (left center) Historic Annapolis office, Shiplap House; (below) Market House and Middleton Tavern

1955 and the gradual restoration of its exterior. The organization was small, however, and had limited funds. At the same time it faced a potentially catastrophic situation, as Annapolis then had little zoning or planning control. In order to maximize its impact with its limited resources, the organization turned to tours, publicity, and historic plaques as a way of awakening the public. For more practical control over changes to historic properties, the organization began a program of obtaining easements for preservation. These were of two kinds: negative easements, which stopped further development of the property; and positive easements, which prescribed restoration to be carried out and maintained on the property. Sometimes the easement was purchased from the property owner, at other times the owner donated the easement to the organization. With the positive easements, Historic Annapolis often provided the drawings for the restoration to follow.

Working through the easements program, tours, and publicity, Historic Annapolis had a gradual impact on the town. While the membership in the organization grew, it faced opposition from a development-minded chamber of commerce and from banks that would not make loans for preservation. In the 1960s Annapolis experienced rapid growth with the location of a new Westinghouse factory in the area and the improvement of highways, which brought Baltimore and Washington within commuting distance. The town population grew from 23,000 in 1960 to 30,000 in 1970.

The rapid growth was both a problem and a resource for Historic Annapolis. The demand for residential accommodation and the desire of local developers to meet the demand created considerable pressure for development in desirable areas and on the waterfront. Most of the new housing was built on undeveloped land outside of the old town, with the great impact on the marshland areas of the four creeks found in the city, but part of the development pressure was felt in the historic area. At the same time, the new residents were often professionals and executives, and were more sensitive to the historic resources of Annapolis. Many supported and joined the work of Historic Annapolis, and some bought and restored houses in the historic area.

In the 1960s, then, the organization faced serious challenges and was to achieve important successes.[2] A modest revolving fund of $65,000 was set up in 1963 and used for both house purchases and easements. In 1965, Historic Annapolis purchased the thirty-five-room Great House of William Paca, which had been threatened with demolition, and began a long fund-raising and restoration effort for the house. But a year later the organization was unsuccessful in court suits to prevent the development of a large modern Hilton Inn on the city's historic waterfront. In scale and appearance, the new building is out of harmony with its surroundings, tending to dwarf the smaller foreground buildings and closing the view along the waterfront. The tension between development and preservation reached a crisis again in 1968 when the city council proposed to demolish the historic Market House facing the city dock in order to add parking space in this central waterfront area. Historic Annapolis's opposition to this proposal resulted in a referendum in 1969 on whether to save the Market House and establish an historical district in the old portion of

FIGURE 6.3 Annapolis: (*above*) Compatible facades; (*below*) Incompatible facades

the town. The voters throughout Annapolis favored saving the market and forming the district. This victory provided preservationists with more control over change in the historical area than had previously existed and had a psychological impact on building owners in the district, who became more sensitive to the historic qualities of their buildings and more open to advice on appropriate restoration. However, Historic Annapolis continued actively to pursue its easement program to insure some legal recourse in case the district commission was pressured into inappropriate actions.

The successes and the setbacks of the 1960s won Historic Annapolis some support in the state government, particularly through the Maryland Historical Trust, which receives state funds and has its own easement program. The banking community, first in Baltimore, then somewhat later in Annapolis, became more open to preservation as property values in the historic area increased and as restaurants and specialty shops in the historic commercial area multiplied on both local and tourist trade. Yet, once again, the very success of preservation brought new problems. As tourism increased, developers turned to this new and profitable market. Today pressure for new tourist facilities on the waterfront continues, and tourist attractions, such as a Naval History Wax Museum, have moved into the historic area. Historic Annapolis has tried to oppose these new developments as they feel they do not contribute to the historic character of the waterfront area, but, as this is often a matter of taste, persuasion has been difficult.

Other buildings of the historic area of the town have been threatened by proposed state government office space expansion and by a city urban renewal project. Historic Annapolis has been successful in persuading the state to consider alternative sites for its new office building, thus preserving the historic integrity of state circle. In the urban renewal area, of seventy historic early nineteenth-century vernacular buildings listed in a 1968 architectural survey prepared for the Renewal Authority, twenty were demolished before 1974 and the fate of another twenty was in doubt. However, the Renewal Authority has also encouraged restoration of some parts of the renewal area.

The situation that Historic Annapolis faces is in flux. State or city officials may act in favor of preservation in one instance, against it in another. While preservation has made considerable headway, the continued growth of the town as a bedroom adjunct to Baltimore and Washington and the active real estate market are undermining further progress. The inflation of values for commercial and residential property, in part a result of successful preservation, has diminished the potential of the easement program and the revolving fund. Further, the inflated prices of commercial property make new owners see redevelopment as the only profitable course to take.

Preservation in Annapolis has followed a path similar to that seen in other small towns—to save a part of the historic past, the organization must think increasingly of the development and planning for the whole. The action of market forces and the modern ability to build easily on a large scale makes the preservation of small buildings and small townscapes a precarious process. Usually preservation efforts focus on single buildings and on the general nucleus of the historic area; however, the preservation organization must now concern itself with the growth and development of the entire town. As the town suburbs grow, the economic pressure for redevelopment of the commercial core increases, and the landscape setting of the historic town is altered. Preservationists are thus forced into common cause with planners and environmentalists in trying to moderate the forces of development. The efforts of environmentalists—to protect the marshlands and creeks of the city from the intrusion of commercial marinas and landfill dumps, to preserve the historic path and trails of the surrounding countryside from the impact of residential subdivisions, to insure the traditional open space and public access to the waterfront that have characterized the town against transfer to exclusive private uses, while at the same time allowing the town to grow—require careful development site planning, deed restrictions, and scenic easements. The problems faced by preservationists and environmentalists are commensurate, and their goals are compatible. The image and identity of the old town of Annapolis can be separated from its landscape setting, but not without threatening to undermine the preservation of the old town. In a large city this is less important, as the landscape setting and topography of the historic core are often only a subject of conjecture. In Annapolis, however, the setting is still visible and can be preserved through the careful planning of future development. Unfortunately, this environmental preservation is more difficult than the control of an historic district, as the landscape setting is scattered throughout the rural and semirural areas around the town; thus the critical areas that should be preserved are not easily selected. In recent years, the techniques needed to make this selection have been developed and applied in regional environmental plans. This usually involves the description of the ecology of the area and the identification of ecologically and visually important areas. As these areas are often not suitable for residential use because of slope, drainage, or soil conditions, residential growth can be planned around them so as to protect the appearance and uses associated with the traditional landscape. On the other hand, without this planning, these areas are usually disrupted through unnecessary grading and dumping, and pointlessly lost to public view and use. The difference between environmentally sensitive subdivisions and those that are not is always striking to the visitor, and the loss to the community from traditional subdivision patterns can hardly be compared with the additional money the developer may have saved.

In Annapolis, environmental preservation has lagged behind the preservation of the historic district. In the 1960s the new residential suburbs and waterfront communities were developed with little planning control, and the development of city parks languished. In 1973 the Annapolis Planning and Zoning office published a report, *Green Annapolis,*[3] proposing a long-term program of park development and open space protection. With the support of Historic Annapolis and other private organizations, a program of this kind could protect the landscape setting of the historic area and provide the parks and open space needed by the community.

Alexandria: Town and Metropolis

The problem of preservation in Annapolis, a town physically separate from neighboring large cities, has an interesting counterpart in Alexandria, Virginia, a town located within the Washington metropolitan complex. In the vicinity of the capital, Alexandria has an architectural legacy of revolutionary and early nineteenth-century buildings comparable only to those of the Georgetown area within Washington. Alexandria, however, is a separate city. Both Georgetown and Alexandria have undergone preservation through the restoration of house museums and private residences since the 1920s. The Historic Alexandria Foundation, created in 1954, was an

FIGURE 6.4 Alexandria

offshoot of the primarily educational Alexandria Association of the
1930s. Alexandria has had an old and historic district since 1946, and
the area has been enlarged over the years to include most of the old
town. The architecture in the district is controlled through an
Architectural Review Board.

Insofar as preservation in Alexandria has been primarily a private
effort, with occasional fund-raising drives or petition campaigns by
the Historic Alexandria Foundation and the Old Town Civic
Association to save threatened buildings or prevent actions adverse to
preservation, it is not unusual. Many residences have been privately
restored, and the commercial spaces of the old town have been
privately renovated as specialty shops and restaurants. Nevertheless,
preservation in Alexandria is unusual in the opposition presented by
the chamber of commerce and by developers. The merchants in the
chamber of commerce, which includes few of those in the old town
shops, have had their stores along upper King Street left out of the
historic district. Despite the success of the specialty shops in the old
town, the upper King Street merchants view preservation as

antithetical to their own prosperity. This would seem paradoxical were it not for the large number of Washington suburban shoppers that might be attracted to a redeveloped Alexandria shopping area along King Street. With these shoppers in mind, the merchants have rebuilt or modernized their stores, and have resisted any further expansion of the historic district. Historic Annapolis has also had difficulties with developers planning to build high-rise condominiums on the Alexandria waterfront as residences for people employed in Washington. As initially proposed, the condominiums were to be immediately next to the historic area and would have dwarfed the smaller buildings. Historic Annapolis was able to arrange a land swap with the developers and, with city cooperation, to move the condominiums a few blocks away from the historic area. However, the waterfront area in and around the historic district, particularly the area occupied by the massive concrete Torpedo buildings formerly used to house federal records and now partially used for art studios, will continue to be subject to plans for new developments. The economic benefits that might accrue from such new building may eventually lead city officials to set aside the objections of preservationists. In these examples, the influence of the metropolis that surrounds Alexandria has made it difficult for preservationists to maintain a distinct identity and townscape for their historic city.

The difficulties that preservationists have faced in Annapolis and Alexandria reflect the lack of a local consensus in favor of preservation such as that which has been achieved in Charleston and Savannah. Both of the latter are sufficiently distant from neighboring metropolises to minimize the metropolitan influence. On the other hand, Annapolis and Alexandria experience a conflict between what is thought to be good for the local community and development oriented toward the metropolis. This conflict tends to work against a local consensus in favor of preservation.

In the past, growing cities have often engulfed surrounding towns and cities, with a consequent loss of identity and autonomy for the newly incorporated areas, but a gain in size and power for the metropolis. Whatever the viability of these urban conglomerates today, it is of interest to the preservationist that restoration often occurs in the older areas of the metropolis that were once independent towns or cities. In New York City, for example, a number of the recognized historic districts are located in the once independent city of Brooklyn. These districts include Boerum Hill, Brooklyn Heights, Carroll Gardens, Cobble Hill, Park Slope, and Stuyvesant Heights. They are primarily residential areas and bear comparison with Alexandria, as they were often restored by exiles from Manhattan who were looking for the kind of residential environment that is hard to find on that island. However, unlike Alexandria, the Brooklyn historic districts are only neighborhoods; their neighborhood and preservation organizations do not aspire to maintain the identity of Brooklyn; and except insofar as their neighborhood is affected, they do not become involved in overall planning for Brooklyn.

Santa Fe: Comprehensive Planning

The potential involvement of preservation organizations in overall

FIGURE 6.5 Park Slope *(Brooklyn)*

town planning has been fully realized in only a few cases; among these is the Old Santa Fe Association of Santa Fe, New Mexico. In preserving the historic character of Santa Fe and participating in planning for limited growth, Santa Fe preservationists have kept in mind the difference between their city and the neighboring metropolis of Albuquerque. Although Santa Fe is the state capital, it has a population of less than 50,000 and has retained a traditional culture and appearance. In contrast, Albuquerque has grown to 250,000 people and has sprawled out in suburban growth of modern appearance. In no small way, the preservation of Santa Fe has been a result of the work of the Old Santa Fe Association and its associate, the Historic Santa Fe Foundation, established in 1961 to administer preservation funds and historic properties and to free the association for a more active role in local affairs. In 1957, the Old Santa Fe Association sponsored an historic zone and architectural style ordinance to preserve the historic core of the city. Despite this, in the following years the association was involved in a number of battles to save houses in the historic zone. In 1960, for example, the city planned to demolish the Nusbaum House to provide off-street parking space near the historic plaza. Preservationists proposed an alternative plan to save the house and place the parking lot behind it; they also raised money to restore the house. However, the alternative plan would have reduced the lot capacity from ninety to sixty cars, and the city proceeded with the demolition. The association returned part of the money it had raised and used the remainder in the purchase of the eighteenth-century Borrego House in 1961.

Throughout the 1960s, the association was involved in defending the adobe houses of the Barrio de Analco first from the expansion of the State Capitol complex and then from the demolition plans of the Urban Renewal Agency. With the exception of the infamous and illegal Sunday afternoon demolition of the Curry House in 1968, they were successful in preserving the Barrio de Analco. These successes and failures have led the association to work for stronger controls in the historic zone. At the same time, the Historic Santa Fe Foundation can purchase buildings as a last resort against demolition.

Efforts to preserve historic houses are a routine matter for all preservation organizations, but the routine concerns of the Old Santa Fe Association include any aspect of change in Santa Fe insofar as it might affect the historic appearance and culture of the town. The association went to considerable effort to arrange a nonstandard

FIGURE 6.6 (*above* and *below*) El Zaguan, Canyon Road—Old Santa Fe Association Office

paving and colored curb design for Canyon Road when the city undertook to pave the street; it also worked to have a new zoning category, Residential Arts and Crafts, applied to Canyon Road in order to protect the studios of artists living in the area. In another case the association opposed a zoning variance request when a small market in the historic zone sought to build a new building across the street from its original location. Alongside these minor concerns, the association has routinely taken a position on requests for zoning change that involve significant changes in land use even if these are beyond the historic zone. After a sprawling commercial and motel development arose in the last two decades along Cerrillos Road, the Albuquerque approach to the city, the association opposed any zoning change that would produce similar conditions on the other approaches to the city.

The growth concerns of the association have gone beyond zoning to support for conservation groups in their effort to maintain air and water quality and to recommendations concerning the impact that satellite town development will have on the water supply and municipal service load of the city. They have also been active in trying to limit residential development on steep slopes in the canyons near the city. Although the association has not actively supported political candidates in the city elections, it has sent the candidates a list of questions on issues of interest to the association and published condensed responses in the organization newsletter. They have also proposed alternative plans for the architecture and expansion of the State Capitol complex and for new road and highway construction in and around the city.

These varied and comprehensive concerns of the Old Santa Fe Association are unusual for most preservation organizations, but indicative of the kinds of involvements that are necessary if the growth of a town or city is to be guided along traditional lines. Many preservationists feel that modern forms of architecture and growth can be compatibly integrated with old buildings and townscape. In Santa Fe, however, many preservationists do not share this feeling, and they have therefore attempted to continue the indigenous architecture and to limit any detriment to the historic character of the city that might result from new suburban growth.

Their success in these efforts has been mixed. Although the historic zone has been expanded from its original limits to include some adjacent undeveloped land, it still covers only a part of the total area of the city. There has been a great deal of construction in typical modern styles beyond the historic zone. Efforts by the association to influence zoning changes and new developments have not always been successful. In the historic zone the architectural controls have produced two results. On the one hand, the visitor often cannot distinguish truly old buildings from more recent buildings done in similar style, and this can produce a feeling of confusion and artificiality. On the other hand, some architects working with the indigenous styles and design elements required in the historic zone have produced residential and commercial buildings of great merit and of an appearance unique to New Mexico. In this, the architectural controls encouraged by the association have sustained a viable Santa Fe style of architecture that complements the historic architecture of the city. Certainly, preservationists can be interested in the continuation of regional architectural styles and regional diversity, as this interest is not incompatible with the architectural past they are attempting to preserve.

The preservation of towns and small cities often raises questions of local identity and culture. In these cases, it is not only a matter of preserving old buildings, but also of preserving the cultural viability of a town or city as an independent entity. It is evident that this will take a preservation organization beyond its usual goals into the arena of planning and growth. Although its first efforts will be devoted to preserving historic buildings and townscape, it may often in its work be drawn into other areas of city design.

7. COMMERCIAL AND PUBLIC BUILDINGS:
Adaptive Reuse

In the preservation of residential neighborhoods and their buildings, commercial and public buildings are only occasionally involved. However, in the preservation of urban areas, these buildings are of central concern to preservationists and pose special problems not encountered in residential neighborhoods. The restoration of an historic house is usually within the means of a private individual or group, but the same treatment for commercial or public buildings is often not. In addition, the usual techniques of preservation, such as landmark designation or inclusion in an historical district, will delay but usually not prevent demolition of a building on a desirable piece of downtown real estate. Purchase of the building by a private preservation group is usually not feasible, and the high cost also deters city officials from using the purchase powers authorized under many landmarks ordinances. In recent years adaptive reuse of large buildings has been developed as a way out of this dilemma and has been particularly successful in areas where pressure for higher density redevelopment is not great. Unfortunately this method will not always work, and the remaining tactics of persuasion and publicity will not often prevail over the economic gain sought in redevelopment.

A single notorious case, the demolition in 1971 of the old Stock Exchange in Chicago, designed by Louis Sullivan and Dankmar Adler in 1893, will illustrate the problems of saving a well-known downtown landmark. The demolition of the old Stock Exchange was no ordinary affair. The building on LaSalle Street, the economic center of Chicago and the Midwest, was unique. It was well known to architects and architectural historians throughout the world. The application to demolish the building was immediately opposed by Chicago preservationists, and the matter was studied by the city government from the Commission on Historical and Architectural Landmarks to the mayor himself. A special committee was appointed by the mayor to review the problem. At least two innovative schemes were proposed to save the building. The developers also presented their case before the city and the public. The controversy was given full coverage in the city news media, attracted national attention, and became a cause célèbre. Yet, in the end, the building was demolished and replaced by a forty-four-story office tower. To understand why the old Stock Exchange was destroyed we must examine the architectural, social, and economic positions occupied by the unique building.

Architecturally, the old Stock Exchange was clearly a building of the first order of importance, a key building along LaSalle Street, designed by two of the major figures of the Chicago school of architecture. The building employed in part an innovative caisson foundation designed by Dankmar Adler and William Smith, whereas the exterior form was the work of Louis Sullivan:

> The exterior form of the Stock Exchange is an organic outgrowth of steel framing without being a direct expression of it. Sullivan abandoned the plastic surface texture of the Wainwright and the Garrick Theater and treated the wall as a repetitive series of largely transparent planes. The general impression made by the street elevations is that of a great box composed largely of glass and poised lightly on the arcade of the third story. On the main portion of these elevations, between the three-story base and the top story, Sullivan scrupulously avoided the use of ornament and refrained from imposing either a horizontal or a vertical emphasis. Throughout its major area, the wall becomes a thin curtain drawn in neutral tension over the projecting bow windows and the flat areas between them. The quality of a skin-like envelope is heightened by the shallow reveals and by the absence of continuous courses or bands, the narrow moldings around the windows forming closed rectangles.[1]

The engineering and design innovations of the Chicago school were unique in their time. Among these, Sullivan's designs are the most elaborate, and often today, the most admired. Despite their importance, Adler and Sullivan, or Sullivan alone, carried out commissions for relatively few major buildings: the Auditorium Building (1887-1889), the Wainwright Buildings (Saint Louis, 1890-1891), the Schiller Building-Garrick Theater (1891-1892), the Transportation Buildings (World's Columbian Exposition, 1893), the old Stock Exchange Building (1893-1894), the Guaranty Building (Buffalo, 1894-1895), and the Carson Pirie Scott Store (1899-1906). Of these buildings, four were in the downtown Loop area of Chicago and had survived until 1960. In that year, the owners of the deteriorated Schiller Building applied for a demolition permit and proposed to build a new parking garage on the property.

The request for demolition of the Schiller Building started a controversy, and the city refused to grant the demolition permit. The city's Commission on Historical and Architectural Landmarks had awarded the building a plaque, but at the time there were no provisions in the landmarks ordinance for demolition delay or public purchase of the building. As the city had no plans to purchase or restore the building, the owners went to court to obtain the demolition permit, which they argued the city had no right to deny them. The superior court judge ruled that the city did have the right to consider aesthetic merits in issuing demolition permits; but on appeal to the appellate court, it was held that the city must either provide adequate reimbursement to the owners for their property or issue the permit. The judge agreed that it was excellent to attempt to preserve a landmark, but that the cost could not be imposed on the private owners. The city could have appealed, arguing that the building was not losing money, but it did not. As the city had no intention of buying the building, and as no private buyer did so, a demolition permit was issued and demolition began in January 1961. Of the four Sullivan buildings in the Loop area, the Schiller Building was the first to be lost; and a decade later, the old Stock Exchange Building became the second. In both cases, as we shall see, aesthetic concerns did enter into the controversy; however, the real issue turned on the question of building profitability and the investment made by the private owners.

Socially and economically, the old Stock Exchange Building served, from its completion in 1894 until the opening of the Board of Trade Building in 1930, as an office building and the trading floor of the Chicago Stock Exchange. It was thus the center of the LaSalle Street financial district. After 1930 it continued as an office building

FIGURE 7.1   LaSalle Street financial district

and never lacked tenants as a result of its past associations and its location on LaSalle Street. In time, this desirable location contributed to its demise. After World War II, the Loop area experienced a building boom along Madison Avenue, and other new buildings were constructed immediately north of the Loop along Michigan Avenue. The LaSalle Street area did not share in the boom, and businessmen began to discuss the need for new buildings along LaSalle Street in order to ensure the viability of the financial district.

By the 1960s, the economic position of the old Stock Exchange was tenuous. It was thought of in the business community as an old office building, with floor-load capacity and wiring inadequate for modern use. Further, it occupied a valuable and prestigious location, where a new office tower would serve the same function more efficiently, accommodate more tenants, and yield a greater economic return. A new building would also revitalize LaSalle Street. These economic considerations were the undoing of the old Stock Exchange. In 1965 the Stock Exchange Building was well maintained and fully occupied; in that year it sold for $1.5 million. In the next five years it was sold again twice, the last time for $7.5 million. A group of developers had acquired the building and surrounding properties with the intention of building a new office tower. They publicly announced their plans in 1970, and the battle to save the building was under way.

In their effort to save the building, preservationists were in a weak position as it had not been officially designated as a city landmark. To be designated as such under the Chicago ordinance, a building had to be recommended to the city council by the Commission on Historical and Architectural Landmarks. The city council then would refer the matter to its Committee on Cultural and Economic Development, which would review the proposed designation and make a recommendation back to the council for a final vote. At the time the demolition controversy over the Stock Exchange Building arose in 1970, the building had been recommended for designation by the commission on landmarks and the matter was before the council committee. Hearings considering the proposed designation were held in April and again in June 1970. The committee heard three differing sets of arguments about the building: one set presented by the opponents of demolition, including members of the landmarks commission, architectural historians, architects, and preservationists; another set of arguments presented by the proponents of demolition, primarily lawyers representing the developers; and a final set of opinions reflecting the city's appraisal of the building, prepared by the city planning department.

At the hearings, opponents of the demolition made the following points in their presentations:

1. The building was a unique architectural landmark worthy of designation; it should not suffer the fate of the Schiller Building (Garrick Theater).

2. The landmarks ordinance provided for a two-stage process—first, designation based on architectural or historic merit; then, at the same time, owner compensation should that become necessary. As the proposed designation of the old Stock Exchange was the first part of the process, the potential cost of compensation should not influence approval of designation. If the designation was not approved for economic reasons, it would negate the entire purpose of the landmarks ordinance and the landmarks commission.

3. Independent appraisal of the building showed that it could return a profit to its owners, based on a realistic estimate of the value of the land and building at $4 million. This suggested that the developers had paid too much for the building.

4. Development potential of the site could be transferred to an adjacent site, perhaps adding to the legal height of an office tower to be built behind the Stock Exchange Building. This solution was proposed by the Chicago AIA. Development potential could also be transferred to a distant site, as suggested in a development rights transfer plan presented by John Costonis. Either solution would decrease the financial impact of designation for the owners of the building.

5. The committee should not be intimidated by the compensation figures presented by the developers.

The proponents of demolition presented the following arguments to the committee:

1. This was not Sullivan's greatest building: it was given a secondary place on the original landmarks commission list. It

had been converted to office use from its original purpose and would be costly to restore. Old buildings die and must be replaced.

2. The building was obsolete and not profitable. It would not produce enough income to cover the minimum ground rental.

3. The developers had entered into lease agreements for $7 million based on demolition of the old building and construction of a new office tower. Financing arrangements were delicate and had to be closed as of November 1, 1970. Further delays would be costly.

4. The independent appraisal did not take into account the $7 million fair-market value of the land and building. This was the figure that would be used for compensation in court.

5. Developers would suffer depreciation on properties they had acquired adjacent to the old Stock Exchange if it were designated, and they would sue the city to recover the loss.

6. Development rights transfer was an interesting idea, but had not been legally instituted in Chicago, and was not feasible in this case. The 30 North LaSalle location of the Stock Exchange was unique and could not be duplicated. Furthermore, the developers could not assemble another parcel on which to use the added development potential.

7. The cost to the city would be $10-$15 million, and even after the building was restored it would be a large white elephant requiring a subsidy every year.

Another set of arguments was presented in a report to the committee prepared by the Department of Development and Planning:

1. Under the urban design heading of the Comprehensive Plan, the building was inadequate because there had been substantial changes from its original use, specifically the Exchange Room had been removed. The building was also obsolete.

2. Under the economic development heading of the Comprehensive Plan, the designation of the building would not economically strengthen LaSalle Street or help in realizing the need for new commercial development.

3. Economic solutions that had been proposed, such as development rights transfer or federal assistance, were not practical.

The members of the council committee chose to take into account the economic side of designation and, with one dissenting vote, they rejected designation of the building. In August, the city council as a whole voted against designation.

Nevertheless, the public controversy continued. In February 1971, the Commission on Historical and Architectural Landmarks again recommended designation of the building. At the end of March, Mayor Daley appointed a special committee to study the problem and withheld the demolition permit until he received its report. The special committee covered the same ground surveyed in the earlier hearings, and in July it recommended that the city purchase the building for an estimated $10-$12 million and resell it to a developer sympathic to preservation. While the mayor and the special committee sought a developer, pleas and proposals continued to appear in the city newspapers. In the end, no developer was found to rehabilitate the building, and city funds to purchase the building were not forthcoming. The demolition permit was issued in October, and demolition commenced. Pieces of the buildings, particularly Sullivan's ornamental details, were sold to various museums. The entry arch and the exchange trading room were subsequently reconstructed as exhibits at the Art Institute of Chicago.

The destruction of the Stock Exchange Building was not inevitable. There was sufficient time to save the building and there was sufficient public sentiment in favor of doing so. The issue was not the architectural merit of the building; rather, it was a question of profit and commercial development. The building had been sold on a speculative basis, and the development group expected a large return on their investment; even if the old Stock Exchange was profitable, it would not yield a large return. The city government also favored new development on LaSalle Street and thus thought its interests coincided with those of the development group. Ironically, both the developers and the city were to be disappointed. After demolishing the old Stock Exchange and building the new forty-four-story office tower, the developers were forced into bankruptcy. The new building has not attracted many tenants, the principal tenant, Heller

International, has even withdrawn, and the city's expectations of commercial revival on LaSalle Street have not materialized.

There are many old buildings of architectural significance in the Loop area of Chicago whose continued existence is as precarious as was that of the old Stock Exchange. To be pessimistic for a moment, there are several factors in the downtown real estate market that are working against the old buildings. Most of these buildings are only marginally profitable, which makes it difficult for their owners to carry out sufficient maintenance. Repairs are often delayed. Since the late 1960s the market for office space has been saturated as a result of overbuilding. The agents for the new buildings offer attractive leases to new tenants, with a consequent loss of tenants in the older buildings. Finally, the current zoning laws allow a height bonus for new buildings that leave a plaza or open space next to the buildings. This encourages the assemblage of several land parcels to provide a large site for both the plaza and the new building and works against preserving the older buildings. In 1975, the Marquette Building by Holabird and Roche, built in 1895, and several adjacent buildings were bought by developers. Demolition to make way for an office tower and plaza seemed likely. However, pressure from Chicago preservationists has for the moment helped to stave off the demolition.

Many of the old buildings depend upon a demand that has developed for architecturally distinctive offices, and this often ensures sufficient tenants for those buildings that are well maintained and in good locations. The Rookery Building on LaSalle Street is a good example of this development; and in another case lawyers active in the new federal court building are finding offices in the Old Colony Building and adjacent old buildings. Several of these buildings have owners or leasing agents sympathetic to preservation, and they have accepted landmark designation for their buildings. Nevertheless, an institutional framework of tax relief or development rights transfer has not been developed to alleviate the economic pressures on the buildings and their owners. Until some avenue of relief is instituted, the preservation of these old buildings will continue to be a problem.

The Chicago Plan and Development Rights Transfers

The problems of saving commercial buildings in Chicago are

FIGURE 7.2 *(above right)* Marquette Building; *(below)* Staircase in the Rookery Building

perhaps unique; there are simply too many architecturally significant buildings. Nevertheless, contemplation of this situation has produced some imaginative and innovative proposals. The Department of the Interior, for example, proposed in 1973 an urban national park composed of several Chicago school of architecture buildings. The late Mayor Daley suggested a nonprofit preservation corporation using both public and private funds. The most interesting proposal to come out of the old Stock Exchange controversy has been the Chicago Plan, an elaboration of the principles of development rights transfers that directly addresses the economic pressures for redevelopment of old buildings in active real estate markets.

Development rights transfers were not pioneered in Chicago; indeed Chicago has yet to adopt any such system. The idea itself is similar to the height bonus allowed on a new building when a plaza or other amenity is established for public use, only the bonus is linked instead to the retention of a landmark building. New York and San Francisco have enacted zoning that allows for the transfer of development rights to a site adjacent to the landmark building. The Chicago Plan, proposed by John Costonis and Jared Shlaes in a 1971 report as a way to save the old Stock Exchange and later refined by Costonis in his book *Space Adrift,* suggests a more comprehensive and far-reaching system of rights transfers than has yet been utilized.[2]

For the details of the Chicago Plan the reader must turn to *Space Adrift;* only a general introduction to this excellent book is possible here. We have seen that in an active downtown real estate market, the economic pressure for higher density development on the land occupied by a landmark building is the major threat to the building. Private preservation groups do not have the funds to purchase such buildings, and the municipal government is in much the same position. These landmark buildings may give their owners a reasonable profit; however, from the owner's point of view, the cost of maintaining the building is often seen in terms of the profit that might accrue from a larger building on the same site. In several recent court challenges to landmark designation, most notably the New York Grand Central Terminal case, owners have argued that their buildings are not yielding a reasonable return and that designation imposes a hardship because they cannot redevelop to achieve a more profitable use of their property. In other words, the owners have argued that landmark designation involves a confiscation of their property. Although the landmark designation of Grand Central Terminal has finally been upheld by the Supreme Court, owners of historic properties will no doubt continue to use the confiscation argument politically to avoid landmark designation.

In order to circumvent this problem, the Chicago Plan proposes a way for the landmark owner to receive compensation for the unused development potential over his building through the establishment of a city-sponsored market for development rights. In this market, the landmark owner could sell the unused potential of his site to a private developer or have the development potential condemned by the city and placed in a municipal development rights bank. The city would in turn, through the rights banks, sell the development rights to private companies. For example, the owner of a ten-story landmark building on a site that allowed a thirty-story building could sell the development rights for the additional twenty stories to the city or to a private developer. These rights would be transferred, as a whole or in part, to a new building being built on another site, and would allow the new building to exceed the height limit on that site. Thus the new building might add ten or twenty stories over the zoned height limit depending on the development rights transferred. The transfer of the rights would be restricted to specific districts in the city, such as the downtown area or other high-density districts specified through the zoning process. In these districts, the density limit on buildings would be set at a level lower than developers might desire. To build larger buildings they would have to purchase the added development rights from landmark owners or from the city. The development rights bank would require start-up funds from the city, but its continued operation would be funded out of the sale of acquired development rights. The bank would also allow the city to market the unused development potential over city-owned landmarks.

Once the development rights over a landmark were sold, the city would receive a preservation restriction, in the form of a deeded interest in the property, from the property owner, which would obligate him and successive owners to preservation of the landmark. At the same time, as the property could no longer be redeveloped, the property taxes would be reduced and the property would no longer be subject to speculative pressures. Any loss in city tax revenue would be made up on the taxes of the new building incorporating the transferred development rights.

For many years, preservationists have proposed tax relief for landmark buildings, but without ways of creating new tax revenues to offset the loss. Similarly, New York and San Francisco have established ways to transfer development rights from a landmark building to adjacent sites owned by the same owner, but without establishing incentives for such a transfer, without providing a preservation restriction or tax relief, and without integrating the transfers into an overall zoning and planning framework. The Chicago Plan brings together these elements in an innovative and flexible approach that shifts the economic burden of preserving landmarks away from preservation groups and city governments to a development rights market that can readily handle the problem at a minimal cost to the public.

The proposals for development rights transfer in the Chicago Plan could prove useful in protecting areas of the natural environment from unnecessary development, as well as aiding the preservation of landmark buildings. However, the measures suggested in the plan, perhaps because they are both innovative and comprehensive, have not met with rapid approval in the business community or among city governments. Some have found the plan to be too complicated, others suggest that the sale of development rights is not adequate compensation, and still others that transfer of development potential away from a unique site would eliminate one of the reasons development was being considered. At present, although the Chicago Plan has not been adopted in Chicago, it is being given a test in Honolulu. This test should provide the evidence to answer various objections to the plan and if successful should bring wider adoption of development rights transfers in our cities.

Adaptive Reuse

Although a comprehensive approach such as the Chicago Plan has not yet been instituted, preservationists have developed a variety of techniques from historic districts to adaptive reuse to ensure the preservation of commercial and public buildings. These techniques have been quite successful in areas where the real estate market is depressed, such as old slum sections of the downtown and adjacent warehouse areas, but they have also been successful in more active market areas when there has been a strong municipal commitment to preservation. In practice, although historic districts are frequently used to provide architectural and legal protection for the buildings, preservationists have turned to making the buildings economically viable, in other words, to adaptive reuse. It is felt that this is the best way to ensure the continued existence and proper maintenance of landmark buildings and to surmount the problem of demolition through neglect.

Adaptive reuse of buildings often occurs quite naturally without the intervention of preservationists. Yet with very old buildings, obsolete warehouses, and outmoded public buildings, reuse may pose unusual problems that require imagination and commitment beyond the routine buying and selling, renting and leasing, repairing and remodeling activities of real estate agencies. In varying contexts and with various types of buildings, sometimes through private effort and sometimes with public commitment, adaptive reuse for preservation has been achieved in cities from Boston to Seattle and San Francisco.

Several elements must be considered in analyzing examples of adaptive reuse. What type of building is being dealt with? Adaptive reuse has been applied to office and commercial buildings, railroad stations, old city halls, court houses, post offices, warehouses, public markets, and factory buildings. How suitable is a building for adaptive reuse? This can depend not only on the type and the location of the building, but on the nature of surrounding buildings, the public recognition of the historic or architectural merit of the building, the suggested use and market for that use, the ownership of the building, and the availability of financing. These factors, combined in a variety of ways, determine the feasibility of adaptive reuse.

Since the late 1960s, preservation of major buildings has shifted from a romantic or philanthropic pursuit to a normal business undertaking. This shift has coincided with the financial success of some pioneer commercial preservation projects and with a rapid increase in the costs of new construction that have made the rehabilitation of older buildings more attractive. Prior to the late 1960s the business community showed a strong preference for the architectural style and engineering efficiency embodied in new office towers and modern shopping centers, but in the last few years a slow reaction has set in bringing a new appreciation, after appropriate renovations, of design features found in older buildings.

Larimer Square, Ghirardelli Square, and Trolley Square

Forerunners of the shift in attitude toward older buildings can be seen in the preservation of Larimer Square in Denver and Ghirardelli Square in San Francisco. Larimer Square, the 1400 block of Larimer Street, composed of commercial buildings from the 1860s and 1870s, was a small portion of the west end of Denver's downtown. In the early 1960s a thirty-seven-block section of the west end, including Larimer Square, was proposed as the Skyline urban renewal area. Most of the buildings in this area were old and deteriorated, and some served as a home for the city's Skid Row. With the exception of Larimer Square and some newer buildings in the renewal area, most of the Skyline area was demolished after 1967. Larimer Square would also have been demolished were it not for a private preservation effort begun in 1964.

Both sides of the 1400 block of Larimer Square were purchased by Larimer Square Associates, a limited partnership of ten individuals brought together by Mrs. Dana Crawford and her husband. Mrs. Crawford had conceived the project and had surveyed suitable buildings in the Skyline area. The buildings on Larimer Street were architecturally and historically significant, in good condition, of reasonable two- and three-story size, and of low market value. Also, both sides of the street were fairly intact. There were other architecturally and historically significant buildings in the Skyline area, some of larger size than the buildings on Larimer, but as novices the Crawfords did not wish to tackle these larger buildings. The rehabilitation intentions of Larimer Square Associates were not made public until most buildings on the street had been acquired; this kept the market values from rising.

Larimer Square was gradually rehabilitated after 1965 as a specialty shopping area and tourist attraction. Design ideas derived from suburban shopping areas, such as open courtyards, galleries, and arcades, were incorporated in the interior renovation of the buildings, while the street facades were returned to their original appearance. Upper stories in some of the buildings were renovated as office space; others were adapted for store or restaurant use.

At the time Larimer Square Associates formed, conventional financing was not available. Denver banks did not have the expertise

FIGURE 7.3 (*above* and *below*) Larimer Square

FIGURE 7.4 Skyline urban renewal area

to evaluate this kind of project, and the small cash flow involved in preservation, compared with the large cash flows for urban renewal, was not sufficient to draw their attention. For the first eight years of the Larimer Square effort, financing was secured by first mortgages, personal guarantees, and double collateral. Only in 1973, after the project had shown success, was a conventional twenty-year loan arranged with New York Life Insurance Company, a firm sympathetic to preservation. In the first years of the Larimer Square project, both business and urban renewal authorities expected it to fail. Not only were they mistaken, but preservation and adaptive reuse have now spread to a commercial and warehouse area adjacent to Larimer Square. But for a few years, the Skyline urban renewal area might also have enjoyed this revival. As it is, Denver has one of the largest and most spectacular downtown parking lots of any American city.

Another trendsetter in commercial preservation was the Ghirardelli Square project in San Francisco, a private effort initiated by William Roth and some associates in 1962. Ghirardelli Square occupies a block complex of old factory buildings, the earliest dating from the Civil War, the majority built between 1900 and the First World War to serve the needs of the Ghirardelli Chocolate Company, which used the complex until 1960. The factory, overlooking the waterfront and the bay, was obsolete, and the threat of high-rise development induced Roth to purchase the property with the intention of preserving the existing buildings. After consideration of various possible uses, it was decided to convert the complex of buildings into a unique quality shopping, restaurant, and entertainment center. The conversion was carried out by the architecture firm of Wurster, Bernardi, and Emmons, with landscaping by Lawrence Halprin and Associates. The design treatment, a clear combination of modern elements (window treatment, stairwells, elevators) with exposed brick masonry structures and interior plazas at several levels separating the buildings, won an Award of Merit from the American Institute of Architects in 1966 and set the style for this kind of commercial preservation. The renovation was completed in 1968.

The conversion of Ghirardelli Square to its present use was a costly venture, and as a pioneer undertaking, would probably not have been possible were it not for the financial standing of William Roth and his associates. The initial purchase of the buildings cost $2.5 million, and

FIGURE 7.5 (*above* and *below*) Ghirardelli Square

the completed project, which included construction of an underground garage, cost in excess of $10 million. As a demonstration
project in preservation and contemporary use, the investors
anticipated little return on their investment in the first years of
operation. Financing provided by Connecticut General Life
Insurance Company used an unconventional formula based on
ecomonic performance of the square.

Ghirardelli Square received nationwide attention and became the
prototype for this kind of adaptive use. Its influence was immediately
apparent in the conversion beginning in 1966 of a Del Monte Fruit
Company cannery, two blocks from Ghirardelli Square, into the
Cannery, another specialty shopping and restaurant complex. In en-
suing years, architecturally similar conversions of brick warehouses
in other areas of San Francisco have been developed as design and
decorative centers and showrooms; notable examples are the Ice
House and the Showroom. Other buildings, first near the Jackson
Square historic area, and then in other areas of the city, have been
adapted for office use. For all of these the design style employed in
Ghirardelli Square has been a prototype; further, it has influenced
adaptive use in other cities as well. The commercial development of
Trolley Square in Salt Lake City is a recent example of the lasting
influence of Ghirardelli Square.

Trolley Square, a shopping and entertainment center, was
developed in the 1970s out of a thirteen-acre jumble of turn-of-the-
century trolley barns, fuel tanks, and barbed wire that once was the
center of Salt Lake City's trolley car system. The developer, Wallace
Wright, recognized the potential of the site—close to downtown, on
a major city thoroughfare, and with large areas for parking—after a
visit to San Francisco and to Ghirardelli Square. He formed a
partnership with seven other businessmen, Trolley Square Associates, which purchased the property for the cost of the land. As
lenders were skeptical about the project, financing depended upon
personal collateral. Albert Christensen of Architects Planners
Alliance designed the conversion of the long trolley barns into a
multilevel, multiaxis specialty shopping center with a turn-of-the-
century theme. The design has encouraged ornately decorated shops
set in intimate spaces and narrow avenues. Artifacts collected from
other buildings are built into the interior facades, along with old
trolley cars and new constructions of stucco, iron, and wood to

FIGURE 7.6   (*above* and *below*) Trolley Square

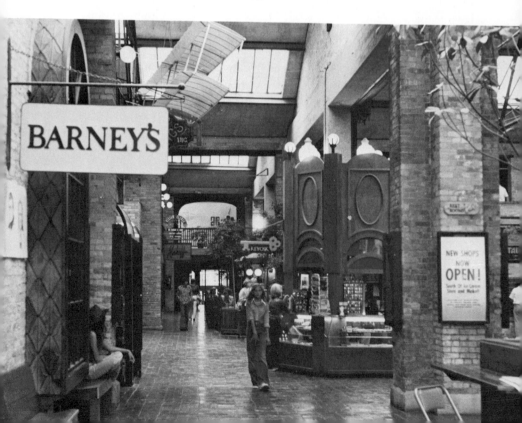

counterpoint the brick of the trolley barns. The overall effect is intended to be complex and inviting, luring the visitor around the corners. The single axis, slick uniformity of conventional shopping centers has been avoided.

When the first portion of the Trolley Square was renovated in 1972, the developers sponsored several events, including a hot-air balloon flight, a charity drive with a radio station broadcasting from the water tower in the square, and flea and farmers' markets in unrenovated parts of the complex, all in order to attract public attention to the square. These activities have established the square as an important tourist attraction in the city with a weekly traffic of 60,000 to 70,000 people. There are eighty shops, restaurants, and theaters in the complex, and the leasable area will be 280,000 square feet when completed. After the square had shown good economic performance, the developers were able to arrange long-term financing with personal guarantees.

Practical Adaptive Reuse in Boston and San Francisco

The success of commercial renovation in Larimer Square and Ghirardelli Square in the 1960s did not go unrecognized by innovative architects and developers, and in the 1970s several firms emerged that specialized in the adaptive use of old buildings. These firms approached adaptive reuse pragmatically based on the experience of the preceding decade. Projects were planned in feasibility studies, conventional construction financing became more readily available, and renovation was speedily carried out to ensure early tenant occupancy.[3]

The renovation of Boston's Old City Hall by Architectural Heritage, Inc., is a good example of pragmatic adaptation of a landmark building. When the Boston city government vacated the Old City Hall in 1970 for its new quarters, public and private attitudes toward the old building were highly ambivalent. Some associated the Old City Hall with past corruption in city government and wanted the building torn down, others favored turning the building into a museum, and a third group suggested conversion of the building to commercial use. Before the building was vacated, the Boston Redevelopment Authority had advertised the availability of

FIGURE 7.7 Boston's Old City Hall

the building for renovation, but no developers expressed interest. A panel appointed by the mayor studied the cost of renovation, estimated from $3 million to $5 million, and did not recommend saving the building. However, Roger Webb of Architectural Heritage, Inc., having done feasibility studies for building renovations, felt that this figure was too high. He submitted a proposal for privately financed conversion and adaptive reuse of the building to the city government. After negotiations, Old City Hall Landmark Corporation, an offshoot of Architectural Heritage, Inc., leased the building for ninety-nine years from the city. The renovation began in 1970, financed by a group of six Boston banks providing $2.7 million in mortgages. The exterior of the building, designed in the second empire style of the 1870s, was cleaned and refurbished. The interior, aside from oak doors and trim, was gutted, and new heating, wiring, plumbing, and elevators were installed producing modernized office and restaurant spaces competitive with neighboring downtown buildings. Only tenants compatible with the image of the building, including a French restaurant and the Massachusetts Housing Finance Corporation, were given leases. Applications from the MacDonald's hamburger chain and from an adult movie theatre were rejected.

The Old City Hall had undeniable advantages that contributed to the success of this conversion to commercial use. It was a well-known building in an excellent downtown location. Preservation sentiment and the market for offices in prestigious old buildings were also well established in Boston. In addition, several Boston banks were willing to finance the project and share the risk even though this was the first conversion development ever attempted by Architectural Heritage, Inc. Finally, the lease from the city was favorable to the nonprofit developers and did not require an initial purchase investment.

A similar conversion project in the same area of Boston, the One Winthrop Square Building, was carried out successfully by Childs Bertman Tseckares Associates under a normal competitive market situation.[4] The experience of converting One Winthrop Square has led the developers to emphasize the need for a rapid and efficient renovation of old buildings in order to reduce high interest costs on construction loans and revenue lost while the building is unoccupied. In their conversion of One Winthrop Square, they attempted to increase the maximum rentable space by utilizing attic spaces and installing mezzanines, and by relocating equipment necessary to the elevator, air conditioning, or other support systems to spaces that could not be readily used for office purposes. Finally the developers completed a model office early in the conversion process that could be shown to prospective tenants, and they worked to complete leased spaces quickly so that revenues from tenants could be used to offset continuing conversion costs. These technical and marketing considerations reflect the economic realities of making a building pay its way and are at the heart of adaptive reuse. Of course, other factors such as location, distinctive architecture, and demand for offices in prestige buildings, all present at the Old City Hall and One Winthrop Square, are also of considerable consequence.

In this sense the preservation situation in Boston and in San Francisco was unique because of the widespread desire for prestige offices and shops in old buildings established in the 1960s. Moreover,

Boston and San Francisco are unusual because of the large number of architecturally excellent old buildings located in the downtown business and shopping areas. In San Francisco the progress of reuse from innovation to accepted practice has been particularly striking, as renovation has spilled out of the Jackson Square Historic District into all areas of the downtown.

The Jackson Square area, composed of small commercial buildings that survived the 1906 earthquake and fire, became a center for the interior design and home furnishing trade beginning in the 1950s. The buildings were converted into showrooms and offices, and the exterior facades were gradually restored to something of their original appearance. This development reflected as much the design sensitivity of San Francisco's interior decorators as it did any quest for historic authenticity. It also reflected the tastes of their clientele who had undertaken the restoration of houses in the Pacific Heights area of the city in the 1950s.

Given the precedent for adaptive reuse provided by Jackson Square and Ghirardelli Square, San Francisco developers have proceeded to renovate and restore buildings throughout the city. A good example of this is the recent renovation of the Hallidie Building by the Conner/McLauglin development firm and the Kaplan/McLauglin architectural firm.[5] The Hallidie Building is a seven-story downtown office building with a glass curtain wall facade designed by Willis Polk in 1918. The decorative ironwork cornices, balconies, and curtain wall framing had originally been printed bright blue and gold, the colors of the University of Calfornia, as the building had been named after a university regent. In later years, however, the ironwork was painted in drabber colors, and the first floor commercial space was unsympathetically remodeled. In the renovation of the building in 1975, Conner/McLauglin used a "fast-track" approach in order to reduce costs. This included retaining some existing tenants in the building and renovating for new tenants on a tight schedule once leases were signed. The developers preferred to attract corporate tenants who would occupy entire floors and thus reduce costs instead of the smaller architectural or design partnerships that are often found in restored buildings and occupy small offices. In their renovation of interior spaces the architects took a no-frills approach, modernizing lighting elevators and other essential equipment, but avoiding costly nonstandard improvements

FIGURE 7.8 (*above* and *below*) Jackson Square

unless paid for by the tenant. After considerable experience in the renovation market, Conner/McLauglin have found that the costs of renovation (twenty to thirty dollars per square foot) when compared with costs of new construction (forty to fifty dollars per square foot) are very convincing when explained to corporate clients. The Hallidie Building has leased renovated space to a bank computer facility, an oil company, and a law firm. The ground floor commercial tenant has been retained, and the restoration of the ground floor facade put off for the future; the remainder of the facade has been restored, with the ironwork once again in bright blue and gold.

Conner/McLauglin have renovated several other buildings of similar size, about 80,000 square feet, using the same approach. Several other San Francisco architectural and development firms are active in the renovation of buildings of this size, as well as smaller ones, and there has also been some adaptive use of even larger buildings, the largest being the conversion of the nearly 500,000-square-foot China Basin Building from a warehouse to an office building. However, to date, adaptive use on this scale has been the exception rather than the rule.

Although one might assume, given the strong preservation sentiment and well-developed system of adaptive reuse, that all is well for preservation in San Francisco, this is not the case. The city has been subject to the same development pressures found in New York and Chicago and has lost some buildings while several more are threatened. The Manhattanization of San Francisco, as it is called, has been encouraged by the city government and business leaders seeking further economic growth. Manhattanization began with the fifty-one-acre Golden Gateway-Embarcadero Center redevelopment project of the early 1960s that replaced a congested old wholesale produce market area with high-rise apartments, office towers, and a hotel. This was accompanied by a building boom in which many San Francisco corporations replaced old office buildings with new towers. The ten-story Crocker Building of 1892 on Market Street was replaced by a thirty-eight-story Aetna Life and Casualty Building. The Bank of America Building, the Security Pacific Bank Building, the Levi Strauss Building, and the Transamerica Pyramid are other examples. Several of the hotels have also added new towers. This is a process that shows little sign of abating in the financial district and along Market Street. In 1975 the twelve-story Alaska

FIGURE 7.9   Manhattanization
FIGURE 7.10   Jackson Square and the Transamerica Pyramid

Commercial Building of 1906 was torn down by the Bank of Tokyo to be replaced by a twenty-three-story tower that will more clearly present the image the bank wants to have in San Francisco. The landmark City of Paris department store building on Union Square, presently vacant, is scheduled for replacement by a new Neiman-Marcus structure. Strong efforts by the Foundation for San Francisco's Architectural Heritage have so far failed to persuade Neiman-Marcus to retain even the most cherished portion of the building housing the interior lightwell and dome. At the same time the Fitzhugh Building also on Union Square is threatened with demolition and replacement by a new Saks Fifth Avenue store. The new department stores are needed on Union Square, but their architecture may not be in harmony with the appearance of the square. However, the older buildings are not suited to the techniques of modern merchandising, and it seems likely that economic considerations will prove to be more important than the architectural status quo.

Many of the buildings lost in San Francisco were not of great architectural or historic significance; they did, however, contribute to both the harmony and rich variety of the city. The buildings that replaced them are often out of scale and of less interesting detail, but they are more profitable and efficient. The Manhattanization of San Francisco has not gone without opposition from preservationists and other groups concerned with the way the city develops. Height limitations on new buildings have been proposed and even presented to the voters in a referendum; but as yet they have not been adopted. In the Alaska Commercial, City of Paris, and Fitzhugh cases adaptive reuse was proposed by the Foundation for San Francisco's Architectural Heritage to the developers with detailed feasibility studies, yet these preservation solutions were not accepted. The decisions to reject adaptive reuse are not based solely on economic factors; they also reflect the desire of the developers involved to project a new image through a new building.

To offset this new building–new image attitude, preservationists need to emphasize the publicity and prestige that can result from restoration of an old building. A case in point in San Francisco, which will be very useful to its preservationists in future arguments over adaptive use, was the extensive publicity that the Chartered Bank of London received when it restored the Merchants Exchange Trading

FIGURE 7.11   Merchants Exchange Trading Hall

Hall as the bank's head office in the Merchants Exchange Building. The basilicalike trading hall designed by Julia Morgan, a rich interior with thirty-eight-foot columns, marble wainscoting, a carved oak ceiling, and large maritime paintings, had served the Merchants Exchange until 1947 when the exchange ceased its operations. New tenants at that time had obscured the old-fashioned painting and oak ceiling with a false ceiling and modern light fixtures. When the Chartered Bank of London leased the hall in 1974, it was not aware of the hidden decorative detail until the building manager arranged a special tour. They decided to restore the trading hall and the paintings to their original appearance at a cost in excess of $250,000. During the restoration the new head office was featured on the cover of *San Francisco Business*. When the office opened, the restoration was featured in the business section of the *San Francisco Chronicle* and used as the subject of a bank advertisement. The bank held a gala opening reception, and during the first week visitors were met by a doorman in Beefeater costume, given color prints of two of the restored murals, and served tea and refreshments. The value of this publicity is hard to estimate, but it is certainly more memorable to the public than the opening of another modern bank office.

Municipal Involvement with Adaptive Reuse: Seattle and Boston

The progress of adaptive reuse from innovation to accepted practice has occurred in Seattle as well as in San Francisco, and further, it has been aided by the active support of the Seattle city government since 1970. Adaptive reuse in Seattle began inauspiciously in 1964 in the skid-row Pioneer Square area when Ralph Anderson, a young architect, bought a deteriorated three-story building for $30,000. Anderson mortgaged his home to finance the purchase and carried out a piecemeal renovation. The second floor of the building was used as his office, the first floor was leased out after renovation to a decorator, and the third floor was remodeled as an apartment. Between 1965 and 1968, Anderson and a friend, Richard White, bought or leased other buildings adjacent to the first one. In this way they were able to coordinate the exterior restorations and use compatible colors and signs. Interior spaces were brought to rentable condition at minimum cost and left for tenants, usually galleries and shops, to finish. Their example was followed by other building owners in the immediate area, and they were also able to arrange for the city to plant some trees along the street and change the street lighting fixtures.

The first efforts in Pioneer Square were carried out at a low cost and investment. The buildings chosen by Anderson and White were small and were purchased at depressed market values on a real estate contract basis. Renovation was done slowly to avoid having to bring the building up to code, old plumbing and wiring were used where possible, and major structural changes were avoided. All of these measures reduced the cost of renovation and the need for conventional financing, and allowed rental rates to be set at an attractive level. However, only a small portion of the Pioneer Square area had been rehabilitated in this fashion prior to the designation of the Pioneer Square Historic District in 1970. After that, the rate of building renovation accelerated, and changes in the market cost of buildings and code enforcement policies brought about more complete renovations using conventional financing. Public investment in street improvements and other amenities increased after 1970.

The transition in adaptive reuse from innovation to accepted practice, and the role of the city government in the outcome, can be seen in the renovation of the Grand Central Building in Pioneer Square.[6] The vacant building had been acquired by Ralph Anderson, Richard White, and Alan Black in 1971. It was a larger building than they had previously renovated, and in worse condition; yet they had proceeded without assurance of financing and without a master plan for the building. While deciding what to do with the building, they had a work crew gut the interior. Their plans for the building were favorably affected when the city bought the half block behind the building for a park; this subsequently became Occidental Park. The city's action turned the building's back facade into a commercially

FIGURE 7.12   Pioneer Square and the Pioneer Building

useful area, and this was incorporated into a ground-floor arcade running through the building from the front entrance to the park. With the upper floors of the building planned for office space, the developers began to seek financing. Their first approach to a bank that had previously made loans in the area was turned down, but their second effort with Seattle Trust and Savings Bank was successful. In the interim another action affected their plans, this time less favorably.

After the 1971 earthquake in Los Angeles, Seattle officials had tightened the enforcement of building code earthquake-safety requirements. As the Grand Central Building was the first major building in Pioneer Square to undergo a complete renovation not extended over several years, it had to be brought up to code. This required a complex structural reinforcement of the previously unreinforced masonry building and added significantly to the cost of renovation. Because of the time lost in planning and financing the rehabilitation and because of the cost overruns, the developers ran out of money with only a part of the building redone and tenanted. However, they had applications for the remaining space at rental rates higher than those used with the initial tenants and were able to approach Seattle Trust and Savings Bank for additional funds. The restoration of the building was completed two years after it was purchased and will not return a substantial profit to its developers until the initial leases expire and are renegotiated at the higher rates now characteristic of Pioneer Square. In many ways, the renovation of the Grand Central Building was a learning experience for the developers. It was the first building in the area to be fully restored, air-conditioned, and brought up to modern standards with conventional financing. It set a new standard for rehabilitation in the area and prepared the developers to proceed efficiently on later projects.

The success of the Grand Central Building renovation, and the city's efforts to upgrade Pioneer Square attracted new developers, such as the Theta Company that renovated the Pioneer Building. Built as a six-story prestige office building after the fire of 1889, of an excellent design combining brick, terra-cotta, and sandstone, the Pioneer Building had been vacant for twenty-five years except for the ground floor storefronts. In 1973 Theta Company studied the need for quality office space near the downtown core and the

FIGURE 7.13 *(left* and *right)* Pioneer Building

feasibility of restoring the Pioneer Building for this purpose. With favorable findings, Theta Company chose the well-seasoned Ralph Anderson and Partners as architects for the project, arranged financing with Great Western Savings and Loan and with Seattle Trust and Savings Bank, and proceeded with a "fast-track" rehabilitation of the building. This included structural reinforcement, a new roof, new mechanical equipment, new glass, cleaning and repair of the exterior facades, and refinishing of interior details. On completion the building was 85 percent leased. The result was a success in terms of both preservation and economics. The Theta Company, long a developer of new buildings, now plans to continue as a developer of old buildings as well.

The Seattle city government made several important contributions to the success of Pioneer Square.[7] The designation of the area as an historic district in 1970 was taken by the business community and others as an indication that the city was committed to the upgrading of Pioneer Square. Through the efforts of Arthur Skolnick, then city conservation officer and manager of the historic district, federal funds were obtained for two new cobblestone parks and a pedestrian mall, and city funds were used for new trees and historic streetlights. A free bus service was instituted linking Pioneer Square with the

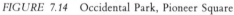
FIGURE 7.14   Occidental Park, Pioneer Square

downtown core. The city government, following a preservation policy applied to the entire downtown, leased office space when needed in existing buildings in Pioneer Square. The city also used model cities funds to purchase a building in Pioneer Square that will be resold for adaptive reuse. Model cities funds and other federal funds were also committed to an Indian Center, a health facility, and the Skid Road Shelter to help the traditional residents of Pioneer Square and adjacent areas. The historic district ordinance was reinforced by the creation in 1973 of a Pioneer Square Special Review District to control land use and by a minimum maintenance ordinance in 1974 to prevent neglect of buildings. As a result of these city initiatives and the private renovation efforts, the tax base in Pioneer Square has risen sharply, the crime rate has declined, and the area has become an important tourist attraction with many shops and restaurants.

In terms of suitability for preservation, the Pioneer Square area was particularly fortunate in the number of buildings of similar architectural style or period concentrated there. With only a few gaps, the architectural fabric was intact, with stylistic motifs carried from one building to the next tying the whole together. Commercial districts with this degree of integrity, once renovated, are particularly impressive. Other cities have also begun to recognize this and to single out intact commercial districts for protection. This is apparent in the efforts to preserve the cast iron buildings of the West Main Street Historic District in Louisville and the twenty-six-block Soho–Cast Iron Historic District in New York.

In these commercial districts preservation efforts have proceeded in a somewhat different fashion. The West Main Street district of Louisville has been a primary concern of the Preservation Alliance of Louisville and Jefferson County, an organization started in 1972. It has publicized the area, encouraged private renovations of buildings, and participated in locating the city's natural history museum and the Junior League in Main Street buildings. The Cast Iron District in New York first came to public attention in the late 1960s when artists began to occupy and renovate as studios and galleries the lofts of the commercial buildings. The city government encouraged this adaptive use by changing the zoning in the area to allow mixed residential and commercial uses. The artist residents and the building owners subsequently sought historic district designation for the area

FIGURE 7.15 Soho–Cast Iron District

as a way of protecting the buildings and perpetuating the new balance of mixed residential and commercial uses. As loft conversions to residential and studio uses accelerated, the demand for loft space surpassed the available spaces in the Cast Iron District. As a result, some of the old commercial tenants have been displaced, the fashion of loft conversions has spread to suitable buildings in adjoining areas of Lower Manhattan, and a new group of firms specializing in the varous aspects of loft conversions has emerged.

These commercial districts shared certain features that facilitated their preservation. The commercial buildings were not isolated amidst incompatible buildings, but rather formed a coherent grouping that could be easily identified. The visitor knew he was in Pioneer Square or the Cast Iron District. Further, a market existed for the space in the renovated buildings, either for commercial, office, or studio uses, and private rehabilitation had begun to occur. Historic district designation and public investment in the area encouraged further renovations. These are the supportive conditions in which adaptive reuse is generally likely to be successful.

The role of the city government in encouraging preservation and adaptive reuse can take a number of forms from city policy statements to direct economic involvement. The Seattle city government took one role in preserving Pioneer Square and another in preserving Pike's Place Market, an old-fashioned public produce market with many stalls and a myriad selection of fruits, vegetables, meats, and fish. Where once these markets could be found in every city, they have become increasingly rare as their economic function has been taken over by supermarkets and produce distribution centers. Often occupying valuable land near the downtown core, they have become prime candidates for urban renewal clearance and redevelopment. In this, Pike's Place Market was no different from its brethren.

Pike's Place Market was created in 1907, prospered until World War II, and subsequently declined. Created as a competitive public market, it offered a wide variety of produce at unregulated market prices; however, as the suburbs grew, the number of shoppers at the market declined. The number of sellers at the market also declined as agricultural land was sold off to urban developers. From a high of 600 merchants before the war selling at the market, the number dropped to 100 in the postwar years. In the early 1960s the city government

FIGURE 7.16 (*above* and *below*) Pike's Place Market

and the Downtown Development Association began to consider the redevelopment of the market via urban renewal. The redevelopment proposal suggested a small museumlike market surrounded by high-rise and condominium developments.

The redevelopment plan was opposed by a citizen's group, Friends of the Market, formed by Victor Steinbrueck, an architecture professor at the University of Washington. While they publicized the local color of the market, the group made little progress in reversing the city's renewal preparations. They finally circulated petitions for a referendum on the fate of the market. The matter came to a vote in 1971, and the Seattle electorate approved a seven-acre market to be preserved in perpetuity. In the face of this electoral decision, the city changed the renewal plan, which had already received federal approval and funding, to include preservation of the market.

The citizen initiative established a twelve-member Historical Commission to control change in the Market Historical District. At the same time the market was part of a larger twenty-two-acre urban renewal project, and under the federal renewal regulations the market buildings had to be brought up to code. In replanning the renewal project to include renovation of the market, city officials and the Historical Commission came to realize that if market properties acquired in the renewal process were sold to private developers for renovation, the character of the market would be permanently altered. In order to insure continuity in the character of the market, the city established a nonprofit public corporation, the Pike's Place Market Preservation and Development Authority (PDA), to acquire market properties from the renewal project and to manage the financial and everyday operation of the market.[8]

The preservation of Pike's Place Market has raised some novel problems. Not only will the architecture of the market, a somewhat chaotic conglomeration of rather humble buildings, be preserved; but also the economic character and ambience of the market, a mix of produce merchants, restaurants, thrift, apparel, gift, flower, and barber shops, and marginal daily arts and crafts renters, will be continued. In other words, both architectural and economic preservation are part of the project. Because three separate agencies, the Pike Project renewal office, the Historical Commission, the PDA, are involved in the effort, there is considerable jurisdictional overlap and room for disagreement. Most of the market area not already in public ownership has been acquired by the renewal project without interfering with the daily operation of the market. Renovation plans, once formulated, are evaluated by the Historical Commission, which wants to keep the market humble in appearance and avoid the fashionable appearance created by preservation in Pioneer Square. The PDA also considers the plans, but is more interested in the potential economic uses of the renovated space. To date, only the Corner Market Building has been renovated through the use of federal funds under the supervision of the Pike Project office. It has subsequently been sold at a loss to the PDA. After the renovation was completed, the Historical Commission criticized the paint color, woodwork, and lighting fixtures used in the restoration as too chic for the market. There was also concern that the kinds of tenants attracted to these renovated spaces would be different from the former tenants.

The PDA, more concerned with strengthening the economy of the market, would like to see the market buildings more quickly renovated using the urban renewal and community development funds scheduled for investment in the Pike Project. Furthermore, although sensitive to the traditional mix of market merchants, the PDA feels that the market is large enough to accommodate new daily sellers of arts and crafts and more established enterprises that could lease the renovated space in the Corner Market Building. At present the market is operating on a subsidy from the city. During the renovation phase there will be an additional subsidy from federal funds to aid the merchants to relocate during renovation and to return to their traditional spaces once renovation is completed. Rental levels on the renovated space will be kept as low as possible so as not to drive out marginal enterprises. But, at some point in the future, the PDA would like to see the market operate with as little financial assistance as possible. For reasons of economic preservation, it is more flexible toward the new merchants in the market, and thus in conflict at times with the Market Merchants Association and the Historical Commission, which favor the traditional sellers in the market.

The final results of the preservation of Pike's Place Market will not appear for some time. The renewal project will bring new office and residential buildings into the area around the market, including some low-income housing in renovated buildings. At present many of the Skid Row indigents have migrated up to the market area as Pioneer Square has been renovated. As the market area is renovated and redeveloped, they will probably move on again. As an experiment in architectural and economic preservation with municipal involvement, the progress of Pike's Place Market should continue to have our attention.

Although the Seattle city government has adopted policies and created public corporations to support preservation and adaptive reuse, it has not necessarily extended these policies to all sections of the downtown core. In the case of Pike's Place Market, preservation was forced on the city by a public referendum. In recent years, the Landmark Preservation Board, created by ordinance in 1973, has been unsuccessful in trying to designate several downtown buildings to prevent their demolition and redevelopment. The efforts of the landmarks board have met considerable resistance from the Downtown Development Association and from the Committee on Responsible Landmarks Preservation, which would like to revise the landmarks board. In brief, the Downtown Development Association, which has considerable influence with the city leaders, would rather see preservation confined to Pioneer Square and Pike's Place Market than extended throughout the downtown area. In 1975, the city council placed a moratorium on new landmark designations; in this, the same economic and political pressures have been at work that we found in Chicago. Downtown building owners do not want to lose the development potential of their property, or they want adequate compensation for the assumed loss resulting from designation. Seattle has not yet solved this problem.

The municipal involvement with adaptive reuse in Seattle can be matched with similar municipal efforts in Boston. The Boston Redevelopment Agency has sponsored the restoration of the historic Faneuil Hall—Quincy Market complex through the urban renewal process. With the exterior restoration completed with renewal funds, the interior renovation of the Quincy Market buildings is being carried out by the Rouse Company, the developers of Columbia, Maryland. Because of its established reputation, the Rouse Company was able to get conventional private financing for this extensive interior renovation. The Boston Redevelopment Agency has also worked with the Massachusetts Housing Finance Agency (MHFA), a state agency, to convert the Mercantile Wharf

FIGURE 7.17 (above) Faneuil Hall; (below) Quincy Market

Building in the renewal area to mixed-income housing and commercial space. The MHFA provided the loan for the conversion. The MHFA has also provided loans for other adaptive use projects, a well-known example being the conversion of the Chickering Piano Factory in the South End of Boston into a mixed-income residential and craft community. This innovative conversion was planned and developed by the firm of Gelardin/Bruner/Cott, Inc. Another MHFA loan financed the conversion of the Lawrence Leather Company complex in Peabody, Massachusetts, into a middle-income residential community for the elderly. These examples of adaptive reuse sponsored by the redevelopment agency and the MHFA are, however, somewhat exceptional. Only a very small percentage of MHFA loans are for adaptive reuse, with some loans devoted to housing rehabilitation and most to new housing construction. The agency has rejected several adaptive reuse proposals because the building location was unsuitable to residential use, or because the interior alteration would be too extensive and costly. Although most cities and states have not reached the point of considering the kinds of adaptaive reuse projects sponsored by the MHFA, the factors of location and suitability for residential conversion should be taken into account in proposing such projects.

The participation of the redevelopment agency in preservation is also somewhat unusual, as in the 1950s and 1960s it actively promoted urban renewal through building clearance. Its involvement with rehabilitation was first in areas where the historic landmark status of the buildings was so well established as to forbid clearance. Only gradually has the redevelopment agency begun to extend preservation to less sacrosanct areas, and preservation-oriented planners in the agency, as in most planning departments in the country, are still a small minority.

Adaptive Reuse: Some Difficulties

The cases of successful adaptive reuse we have been examining have often been carried out with old public buildings that have lost their function or with old commercial buildings in deteriorated areas. However, attempts to rehabilitate similar buildings in other cases have not always been successful. In Saint Louis, for example, there is at present a downtown post office building, like Boston's Old

City Hall, waiting for reuse; a railroad station, similar to one successfully converted to a hotel and restaurant complex in Chattanooga, waiting for a developer; and a warehouse district, Laclede's Landing, targeted for renovation. Saint Louis preservationists and business leaders have been trying to start adaptive reuse in these buildings, but progress has been slow, and proposed plans have often fallen through. There are several reasons for the difficulties. In Boston, Seattle, and San Francisco the city residents use the downtown areas that have remained economically strong. In

FIGURE 7.18   Old Post Office Building, Saint Louis

Saint Louis the downtown area has suffered a decline as residents have shifted to suburban shopping centers. The post office and even more the train station are large buildings that will require a major investment to convert to new uses. Laclede's Landing, where there are smaller warehouse buildings, has been partially cut off from the downtown by a freeway and a bridge approach. Even if the railroad station or the Laclede's Landing buildings were renovated, the problem of marketing the space and attracting customers would remain. For the Old Post Office there are currently plans for the federal General Services Administration (GSA) to promote the renovation of the building for mixed public and commercial use. In the case of another downtown landmark, Adler and Sullivan's Wainwright Building, the Missouri state government has purchased the building for renovation as a state office building. The GSA and the state government will find uses for the space in these renovated buildings, but for adaptive use in other buildings in the downtown the problem goes beyond renovation and financing to the need to attract small businesses, customers, and professionals back to the downtown area. Without the kinds of businesses and customers found in preservation districts in Seattle or Boston, it is difficult to see how commercial reuse will be successful.

The decline of the downtown core is not unique to Saint Louis. Other cities have underused old schools, movie theaters, courthouses, and office buildings. Sometimes these buildings can be converted to new uses related to their old functions. The Paramount Theater in Oakland and the Fox Theater in Atlanta have been refurbished as civic performing arts centers. Railroad stations in San Diego and Seattle are being adapted as multimedia transportation centers. Schools and courthouses can be renovated for office use. However, there must be some demand for these new uses. If they duplicate existing services or if there is little demand, the adaptive reuse may prove unwarranted. Through publicity, preservation can to an extent produce public interest in the downtown area. It is doubtful that preservation alone can reverse the decline of a downtown area; but in conjunction with other changes such as new businesses, restaurants, entertainment attractions, and crime prevention, an improvement in the downtown image can occur.

The preservation of commercial and public buildings is an undeniably complex undertaking affected by economic and social factors that may be foreign to the historic and architectural interests of many preservationists. It is easy to wish that an interesting old building will remain where it is, a part of its city's ambience and history, a reference point, a landmark for both the resident and the visitor. It is quite another matter to ensure that this will be so.

It is natural for a city to grow and change, and for new buildings to replace old. Unfortunately, those large buildings that are often most important to us may be outmoded and occupy valuable land. Unless new and profitable uses for them can be found, they will disappear. Of course, some may be saved for public use, and others have survived so long that they are sacrosanct, but the majority cannot be preserved in this way. Their survival must depend upon either private resources or adaptive reuse.

8. CONCLUSION:
Contexts and Functions of Preservation

In recent years the movement for preservation of historic architecture has steadily gained public support. As it has grown, the movement has redefined its goals and refined its techniques, expanding its undertakings from single houses to historic areas and neighborhoods, to towns and large public and commercial buildings. Increasingly, those involved in the movement speak not of historic preservation, but simply of preservation. Their conception of what they are doing has become less specific, more general, more encompassing.

In one sense, preservationists have broken free from the criteria of great age and historic fame used in determining what buildings should be preserved. This change in attitude—and consequent expansion of the scope of preservation—has been a reaction to the postwar building boom that spread suburbs around the historic core of almost every American and European city. It has also been a reaction to the technological revolution in architectural engineering that has made possible new construction and demolitions of unprecedented proportions. Furthermore, this technological revolution has made many older buildings appear obsolete. Repeatedly, preservationists have witnessed the wholesale clearance of renewal areas and the demolition of major buildings; these shocks have led them to redouble their efforts to save what remains.

When the movement for historic preservation began, its concern was for the ancient monument or the old landmark building. Today it seeks to preserve vernacular and humble buildings as well as monumental, and it is not troubled if these buldings are only forty to fifty years old. In some cases even more recent buildings draw its

FIGURE 8.1 Twentieth-century cityscape—Boston

attention. The broad concerns of contemporary preservationists reflect their recognition that almost any building built prior to World War II may be architecturally unique. The materials, the details and craftsmanship, the styles—all are difficult to obtain today or only available at great expense. If we wished, we could not afford to rebuild the variety of structures of the nineteenth and early twentieth centuries that continue to exist in our cities. Some of these have been saved, others have deteriorated and will probably be lost; but, taken altogether, it is the finite number of these buildings that moves the preservationist to save as many as possible. The cityscape of the late twentieth century has already dwarfed all preceding ones;

it is no longer a matter of saving a building here and there, but of saving a cityscape of finite proportions from the massive urbanization of the present.

For preservationists to succeed in saving the cityscape or townscape of the past they must know what is feasible and what is suitable; they must know what will be successful and what alternatives to fall back on should their first efforts fail. To know these things, individual preservation groups must learn to read their towns and cities so that they can recognize what can be preserved. This reading is not simply a matter of history and architecture, or of appropriate restoration techniques, but also of complex social and economic factors that determine the situation in which preservation will or will not occur. We can easily recognize the kind of house that can become an historic house—it must be associated with the rich or famous, or be the oldest house in an area, or be the site of great events—but there are other factors that will come into play before it is preserved. There must be a group with sufficient funds interested in preserving the house; there must be a suitable new function found for the house as a museum, office, or some other use; and there is cause for hope if the general public knows about the house and supports its preservation. On the other hand, the house may be in a poor location for public visits; it may be surrounded by incompatible architecture that detracts from its appearance; its size may make it too expensive to restore and maintain; it may occupy valuable land that developers want for other purposes; preservation groups may have committed themselves to other projects; and, finally, the general public may not care about the house.

In attempting to preserve an historic district, success or failure may be determined not only by these factors affecting individual buildings, but also by matters affecting the area as a whole. An historic district usually must be unique and must contain a relatively complete set of historic buildings. The district should have the potential for tourist or residential appeal, and both residents in the district and officials in the city government should support the preservation of the area. It is an advantage if lenders can be found to finance restoration in the district; it also helps if the district has received citywide attention because it contains an art colony or attractive stores and restaurants. However, if many of the historic buildings have been demolished, if the location is unattractive, if there is too much crime, if the city has other plans for the area, if property owners are not sympathetic, then preservation in the district may not be successful.

When we seek to preserve a neighborhood, although many criteria are the same as those for an historic district, there are additional considerations. The architecture of a neighborhood may not need to be as distinguished or unique as that found in an historic district proper, yet there may be special qualities to the community that the preservation group will want to save. The presence of community organizations and enthusiastic young professional families will help in this effort. Clear neighborhood boundaries and local shopping areas are an asset. The public image of the neighborhood can be an important factor. Conversely, if the houses are too large and deteriorated, if the neighborhood is redlined, if a highway or major traffic artery divides it, or if the residents are too poor, it will be difficult to preserve the neighborhood.

The values that lead to the preservation of neighborhoods are also at work when trying to maintain the identity and traditional character of a town or small city. They may have historic houses and historic districts—these make the task easier. But beyond the historic areas, continuation of a style of life, a culture, and a townscape is sought in these towns. The support of the local social elite for preservation is critical in such cases. If they are opposed to preservation, or in favor of development, there may be little that can be done. In other cases, where a town is near a metropolis, the town's population may be changing, and the newcomers may be open to preservation. However, the new growth will also increase the pressure for new development. In this way, preservation in towns is subject to a favorable arrangement of social factors and to the educational and publicizing efforts of preservation organizations.

Finally, when we turn to the preservation of the monuments of urban culture, the large commercial and public buildings, we find a new set of conditions affecting the course of preservation. Although these buildings often embody architecture and history of great civic significance, they also often pose great economic problems for their admirers. Saving such buildings will be supported if their significance is clearly understood by the public, if they are adaptable to modern uses, and if the city government is committed to their preservation. It will be a great aid if the land they occupy is not highly valued or desired for redevelopment. When these conditions are reversed the preservation of the building becomes difficult. At times commercial and public buildings will be found among others of similar age and architecture, and this situation may serve as the basis for an historic district. More frequently, the large older monument stands with buildings of differing ages and styles, and in this case the preservationist may try to showcase the older building so that it complements and is complemented by its newer surroundings. In either case, the deterioration of surrounding buildings will have an adverse effect on the restoration project, and so rehabilitation of the surroundings must also be encouraged.

Preservation is concerned with both history and architecture, but, more than that, its task is the preservation of the remains of an earlier civic culture. The aesthetic of preservation does not interfere with the development of the modern city, rather it supports it in symbolic, economic, and social ways. The symbolic function of preservation is threefold: the restored buildings acquaint us with the past of modern society; they suggest the direction in which society has changed; and they reveal aesthetic possibilities, through architecture, interior design, and historic displays that enrich modern sensibilities. Economically, restored buildings and historic districts play a significant role in the tourist industry. They are also being successfully adapted for modern uses as commercial shopping areas and offices. This reuse of old buildings is a practical conservation of existing materials. Socially, preservation helps to integrate the society as a whole by serving as a positive and public example of valued life-styles, as seen in the displays in historic houses and in the contemporary examples set by people living in historic areas. Preservation can also help to integrate neighborhoods and towns by providing a focus for community efforts, a reason for involvement and commitment, and thus a way toward neighborhood re-habilitation.

For both communities and society as a whole, the historically accurate restoration of a house or district sets a standard of authentic performance and appearance against which modern activities and the modern cityscape can be measured. In the appearance of modern society, the aesthetic of newness is predominant. Remnants of the old-fashioned past are either destroyed, placed in museums, or adapted for current uses. In museum use, the old building sets a standard for comparison with the modern building, so that one or the other may be judged better or worse. In adaptive use, older buildings undergo a conversion to modern use inspired in part by nostalgia and in part by practical considerations. Through preservation, the past comes to serve the present and contributes to the development of the modern city. In the destruction of old buildings, the contribution of the past is lost.

NOTES

Chapter 1

1. William Morris, speech to SPAB General Meeting in 1884, quoted in the Society for the Protection of Ancient Buildings, *Report of the Committee for the Eighty-Ninth to Ninety-Second Year 1966-1969* (London: SPAB, 1970), p. 9.

2. *Encyclopaedia Britannica,* 11th ed., s.v. "monument."

3. G. Baldwin Brown, *Care of Ancient Monuments* (Cambridge: University Press, 1905), p. 16.

4. Ibid., p. 18.

5. *Christian Science Monitor,* 24 February 1972, p. 5.

6. Lionello Venturi, *History of Art Criticism* (New York: E. P. Dutton, 1964), p. 213.

7. Edward Gibbon, *Decline and Fall of the Roman Empire,* vol. 2, p. 315, quoted in Jacob H. Morrison, *Historic Preservation Law* (Washington: National Trust for Historic Preservation, 1965), p. 1.

8. Stephen W. Jacobs, *Architectural Preservation: American Development and Antecedents Abroad* (Ann Arbor: University Microfilms, 1967), p. 51.

9. Anonymous, *A New Guide to Rome* (Terni: Fotorapidacolor, 1971), p. 120.

10. Robert of Clari, *The Conquest of Constantinople,* in Elizabeth G. Holt, ed., *A Documentary History of Art,* vol. 1 (Garden City: Double-day Anchor Books, 1957), p. 81.

11. Alma S. Wittlin, *The Museum* (London: Routledge and Kegan Paul, 1949), p. 12.

12. Holt, *Documentary History of Art,* vol. 3, pp. 273-74.

13. Alexander Lenoir, *Museum of French Monuments,* in Holt, ibid., p. 277.

14. Paul Leon, *La vie des monuments francais* (Paris: A. and J. Picard, 1951), p. 80. Accounts of French preservation written in English rely heavily on this authoritative source.

15. Jacobs, *Architectural Preservation,* p. 76.

16. Walter J. Hickel, "Foreward," in Michael Frome, *Kodak Guide to Colonial America* (New York: Popular Library, 1970), p. 5.

17. A. W. Raitt, *Prosper Mérimée* (London: Eyre and Spottiswoode, 1970), p. 138.

18. Jacques Dupont, "Viollet-le-Duc and Restoration in France," in National Trust for Historic Preservation, *Historic Preservation Today* (Charlottesville: University Press of Virginia, 1966), p. 15.

19. Raitt, *Mérimée,* p. 153.

20. Dupont, "Viollet-le-Duc," p. 12.

21. Prosper Mérimée quoted in Raitt, *Mérimée,* p. 147.

22. Paul Leon quoted in Dupont, "Viollet-le-Duc," p. 20.

23. John Ruskin, *The Seven Lamps of Architecture* (New York: Noonday Press, 1961), pp. 184, 185-6.

24. Kenneth Clark, *The Gothic Revival* (Harmondsworth: Penguin Books, 1962), p. 64.

25. Ibid., p. 139.

26. Ibid., p. 156.

27. Sir James Summerson, "Ruskin, Morris, and the 'Anti-Scrape' Philosophy," in National Trust, *Historic Preservation,* pp. 30-31.

28. Jacobs, *Architectural Preservation,* pp. 115-16.

29. For a review of the various enactments see G. Baldwin Brown, *The Care of Ancient Monuments* (Cambridge: University Press, 1905).

30. UNESCO publications, the Museums and Monuments Series, particularly A. Noblecourt, *Protection of Cultural Property in the Event of Armed Conflict* (Paris, 1956), and UNESCO, ed., *The Conservation of Cultural Property, with Special Reference to Tropical Conditions* (Paris, 1968).

31. Peter Michelsen, "The Outdoor Museum and Its Educational Program," in National Trust, *Historic Preservation,* p. 203. For a discussion of the reconstruction of war-damaged buildings and an example of preservation in a communist country, see Stanislaw Lorentz, "Reconstruction of the Old Town Centers of Poland," in the same volume.

32. Mats Rehnberg, *The Nordiska Museet and Skansen* (Stockholm: Nordiska Museet, 1957), p. 74.

33. Ibid., p. 122.

34. Michelsen, "Outdoor Museum," p. 207.

35. Charles B. Hosmer, Jr., *Presence of the Past* (New York: G. P. Putnam's Sons, 1965), p. 36.

36. Ibid., p. 57

37. Anne H. Warton, National Society of Colonial Dames of America, quoted in Hosmer, *Presence of Past,* p. 138.

38. Joseph Judge, "Williamsburg, City for All Seasons," *National Geographic,* December 1968, p. 793.

39. Jacobs, *Architectural Preservation,* p. 222.

Chapter 2

1. Laurence V. Coleman, *Historic House Museums* (Washington: American Association of Museums, 1933), pp. 16-17.

2. Ibid., p. 19.

3. Nicholas Zook, *Museum Village USA* (Barre, Massachusetts: Barre Publishers, 1971), p. 43.

4. Special Committee on Historic Preservation, United States Conference of Mayors, *With Heritage So Rich* (New York: Random House, 1966), p. 52.

5. Carolina Art Association, *This Is Charleston* (Charleston: Carolina Art Association, 1944), pp. 51-53.

6. City of Charleston, *Zoning Ordinance* (Charleston: City of Charleston, 1973), p. 32.

7. Ibid., p. 32.

8. Ibid., p. 33.

9. Isabel E. Callvert, "Historic Charleston," *Gourmet,* April 1976, p. 38.

10. National Trust for Historic Preservation, *Annual Meeting* (Washington: National Trust for Historic Preservation, 1970), p. 12.

11. Louisiana Constitution of 1921, Section 22, A., as added by Act 139 of 1936.

12. Ibid.

13. Vieux Carré Commission, *Report 1970-1974* (New Orleans: Vieux Carré Commission [1974]), p. 7.

14. Ibid., p. 6.

15. Robert Tallant, "Introduction," to Lyle Saxon, *Fabulous New Orleans* (New Orleans: Robert L. Crager & Co., 1928), p. xii.

16. William Spratling and William Faulkner, *Sherwood Anderson and Other Famous Creoles* (Austin, Texas: University of Texas Press, 1966), foreword.

17. Bureau of Governmental Research and City of New Orleans, *Plan and Program for the Preservation of the Vieux Carré* (New Orleans: Bureau of Governmental Research, December 1968), p. 35.

18. Oliver La Farge, *Santa Fe* (Norman, Oklahoma: University of Oklahoma Press, 1959), p. 231.

19. Ibid., p. 288.

20. Pearl Chase, "Bernard Hoffman—Community Builder," *Noticias,* Summer 1959, p. 16.

21. Ibid., pp. 20-21.

Chapter 3

1. Jacob H. Morrison, *Historic Preservation Law* (Washington: National Trust for Historic Preservation, 1965).

2. For a discussion of the formation of the Swiss Avenue District see: Lyn Dunsavage and Virginia Talkington, *The Making of a Historic District, Swiss Avenue, Dallas, Texas* (Washington: Preservation Press, 1975).

3. Philadelphia Redevelopment Authority, *Old and Historic Houses in Philadelphia* (Philadelphia: Philadelphia Redevelopment Authority, n.d.), p. 4.

4. Philadelphia Food Distribution Center, *How Philadelphia Created the World's First Complete Food Distribution Center* (Philadelphia: Food Distribution Center, n.d.), p. 18.

5. Philadelphia Redevelopment Authority, *Historic Houses,* pp. 7-8.

6. "Where Urban Renewal Brings History to Life," *Business Week,* 23 October 1965.

7. City of Charleston, *Historic Preservation Plan* (Charleston: City of Charleston, June 1974).

8. Bureau of Governmental Research and City of New Orleans, *Plan and Program for the Preservation of the Vieux Carré,* December 1968.

9. Vieux Carré Commission, *Report 1970-1974* (New Orleans: Vieux Carré Commission [1974]), p. 14.

10. Governmental Research and New Orleans, *Vieux Carré,* p. 58.

11. F. Monroe Labouisse, Jr., "The Death of the Old French Market," *New Orleans,* June 1975, pp. 77-78.

12. Ibid., p. 78.

Chapter 4

1. Arthur Ziegler, Jr., Leopold Adler II, Walter C. Kidney, *Revolving Funds for Historic Preservation: A Manual of Practice* (Pittsburgh: Ober Park Associates, 1975), p. 64.

2. Thomas G. McCaskey, *The McCaskey Report—Savannah, Georgia, as a Travel Destination* (Savannah: Historic Savannah Foundation, 1965), p. 5.

3. Housing Authority of Savannah, *Historic Preservation Plan* (Savannah: Housing Authority of Savannah, 1968).

4. Savannah Landmark Rehabilitation Project, Inc., *Project "SNAP" (Savannah Neighborhood Action Project) Proposal* (Savannah: Savannah Landmark Rehabilitation Project, Inc., 1975).

5. Roy Lubove, *Twentieth-Century Pittsburgh* (New York: John Wiley & Sons, 1969), p. 121.

6. Ziegler, *Revolving Funds,* p. 78.

7. Joe T. Darden, *Afro-Americans in Pittsburgh* (Toronto: D. C. Heath and Co., 1973).

8. Ziegler, *Revolving Funds,* p. 79.

9. Arthur P. Ziegler, Jr., *Historic Preservation in Inner City Areas* (Pittsburgh: Ober Park Associates, 1974), p. 50.

10. Pittsburgh History and Landmarks Foundation, *Old Post Office* (Pittsburgh: Pittsburgh History and Landmarks Foundation, n.d.).

Chapter 5

1. See John Codman, *Preservation of Historic Districts by Architectural Control* (Chicago: American Society of Planning Officials, 1956).

2. Boston Redevelopment Authority, *Charles Street Report* (Boston: Boston Redevelopment Authority, May 1974).

3. Greg Holzhauer, "The Elastic Square," *LaFayette Square Meter,* June 1974, p. 11.

4. Old Town Restorations, Inc., *Building the Future from Our Past* (Saint Paul, Minnesota: Old Town Restorations, Inc., 1975).

5. *Risorgimento,* January 1975, p. 11.

Chapter 6

1. Robertson E. Collins, "Jacksonville, Oregon," *Historic Preservation,* October-December, 1969.

2. Historic Annapolis, Inc., *The Incredible Change* (Annapolis: HAI, 1969) and *For the Next 200 Years* (Annapolis: HAI, n.d.).

3. Annapolis Planning and Zoning Office, *Green Annapolis* (Annapolis: Annapolis Planning and Zoning Ofice, 1973).

Chapter 7

1. Carl Condit, *The Chicago School of Architecture* (Chicago: University of Chicago Press, 1964), pp. 137-38.

2. John J. Costonis, *Space Adrift* (Chicago: University of Illinois Press, 1974).

3. See National Trust for Historic Preservation, *Economic Benefits of Preserving Old Buildings* (Washington: Preservation Press, 1976).

4. Charles N. Tseckares, "Adaptive Office Space in Old Buildings," in National Trust, *Economic Benefits.*

5. Herbert McLaughlin, "Commercial Renovation Proves Its Worth," *Historic Preservation,* October-December 1975.

6. Alan F. Black, "Making Historic Preservation Profitable—If You're Willing to Wait," in National Trust, *Economic Benefits.*

7. Wes Uhlman, "Economics Astride," in National Trust, *Economic Benefits.*

8. City of Seattle, *Pike Place Design Report* (Seattle: City of Seattle, June 1974).

Index

37-38

81
92

180
194
211